HIS INTERPRETERS

HIS INTERPRETERS

*A book for the dawning and the closing
of the day*

by
RITA F. SNOWDEN

LONDON : THE EPWORTH PRESS

THE EPWORTH PRESS
(FRANK H. CUMBERS)
25-35 City Road, London, E.C.1

MELBOURNE   CAPE TOWN
NEW YORK   TORONTO

SET IN MONOTYPE PLANTIN AND PRINTED IN
GREAT BRITAIN BY THE CAMELOT PRESS LTD
LONDON AND SOUTHAMPTON

For

M. L.

My Friend of 'St Christopher's'

Contents

7

His Interpreters

READING: Psalm 19[14]

The little French village cupped the sunshine, and the people went about their work. It was quiet. Their thoughts were not often above their bodily needs. But there was one man in the village of Grez for whom the sunshine and the hills had no loveliness. He was blind. And he was crippled—crippled and blind, and his heart was full of dreams.

Frederick Delius the composer had wandered far before he had come to Grez. With his wife at his side he had tried to be happy and settle to his work; but it was no use. The days were long, and there was no creative joy in them. For years he had applied himself to the high task of capturing for men and women some of the world's loveliness.

Now he could do no more. He sat in the darkness with his dreams; he could move his body only when strong arms held him; he could talk only in whispers. Beside him lay his folder of unfinished manuscript.

Then the miracle happened. News of his plight got out—out to music-lovers afar: 'Frederick Delius is crippled and blind, and his work is not finished.'

To a young man in England—Eric Fenby—it seemed an intolerable thing that a master musician should live in the darkness with some beautiful thing and have no means of bringing it to life.

Surrounded by the health-giving air and space of Yorkshire, the young man took his dog, and walked miles along the cliffs. Surely someone could think of a way. But there was no one to give answer, and the only plan he could think of seemed foolish.

But he took pen and paper and wrote a letter to a little village he had never seen: 'Let me come and try,' said he. 'It might work.'

So Eric Fenby found his way to Grez, to offer his willing eyes, and his willing strength, and his musical gifts to the master.

At first there were obstacles to overcome, but by the end of six months the master musician was dreaming his music aloud. Young Fenby, to the advantage of the whole world, had become the interpreter of the master musician. In a short time the master was saying: 'My dear boy, you finish my sentences for me.' And for six years the wonderful partnership continued until all was finished and the master had said in music all that he wanted the world to know.

Today, the greatest Master of all needs interpreters—ordinary, wide-awake people to make His dream of full and joyful life understandable.

He needs urgently an interpreter in my office, my school, my workshop, my home.

MORNING PRAYER

O Lord of Life, I kneel in Thy presence in this morning hour, that my first response may be to Thee; for many voices distract me as the day goes on.

O Lord, Thou hast lent me my body for life; let me keep at a distance this day all that would mar its fitness and freshness and strength.

Thou hast lent me my mind for thought and for the treasuring of things true and honest, just and pure—all that is lovely and of good report.

Thou hast lighted within my spirit a flame that will never go out. But often it flickers, and there are times, I confess, when it goes untended. Forgive me.

I rejoice that Thy hand is upon the whole of my life. Let me live, this day, to the full; that I may be an interpreter of Jesus Christ to those with whom I have to do.

Strengthen my will to serve, deepen my love, and set some laughter upon my lips; for Jesu's sake. *Amen.*

EVENING PRAYER

Gracious Lord and Master, as the night draws about me and the noises of the busy day are hushed, accept, I pray Thee, the offering of this day.

Forgive me for any failure to interpret the living spirit of

Jesus; for any duty shirked, any harsh word spoken, the harbouring of any unworthy thought. Let me keep nothing from Thee while I pray; lest with some sin unconfessed, I lack Thy full forgiveness.

I bring Thee my thanksgiving for all the rich things of this day—the work I have had to do and the strength to do it, the trust and confidence of friends, the beautiful things that have stirred my heart. I bless Thee for new thoughts that have visited my mind, and new visions of sympathy and service which I have glimpsed.

I pray especially for all those who have urgent need of Thy love this night—the sick and the weary, the discouraged, all those in sorrow, those separated by long distances from those they love.

I pray especially for those who have grown bitter and cynical, and have lost their way. I pray for those who this day have used the good things of the world—the powers of the earth, the sea and sky, all the secrets of science—for the destruction rather than the up-building of life. Forgive them, and lead us past our costly, hurtful ways of human pride and self-glorification into a clearer sense of lasting values. We are frail, and faltering and full of sin; but Thy love knows no end, and was never more near. *Amen.*

He Passed This Way

READING: Psalm 138⁶⁻⁸

As we walked in Cumberland under the stars my old friend and I talked of Waddilove School and John White.

I did not ask about John White's academic qualifications. I did not learn his particular theological emphasis. Only one thing was clear: the foundations of Waddilove School lay in the love and lowly service of John White of Cumberland. He went out to Southern Rhodesia, and began by gathering a few native boys into a mud hut. On that foundation Waddilove School has grown.

Principal for many years, John White wore himself out. The privilege of life was a continual wonder to him. His service ended in 1933, when he was sixty-seven; but it was not length of days that one remembered about John White.

The doctors ordered him back to England, but some of the native boys wrote a letter begging that he might be allowed to stay. In their letter they said a lovely thing: 'We trust him so much, that we take everything of ours to him. . . . There is a little bell at the door of his office which natives ring to announce their presence. And when that is rung he comes to the door so promptly that one would think he came to greet a king. The bell rings so often during the day, and every day, that even the most humble man of any colour would be annoyed, but not Mr White. No native is too low for him to shake hands with.'

I doubt whether John White ever thought out that lowliness of heart, as we did when speaking of him. It was as natural to him as it was remarkable to the boys who remembered him for it.

But there was one thing that John White thought on a great deal, and that was the wonder that the great God should reach down with grace and mercy to the 'low lintel of his human heart'. He had no words adequate to express it—only a life of service. But he pondered often the peerless words of the Psalmist: 'Though the Lord be high, yet hath He respect unto the lowly: but the proud He knoweth afar off.'

And he answered the little bell.

MORNING PRAYER

Not to the wise, O Lord, nor to the prudent,
Dost Thou reveal Thyself, nor to the art
Of the logician keen, and coldly student,
But to the patience of the pure in heart.
Low is the lintel of Thy truth, and lowly
Mortals must bend who fain would see Thy face;
Slow from the darkness dawns the day, and slowly
Sinners ascend into Thy dwelling-place.

I bless Thee, O Lord, for humble hearts who have brought to the daily tasks of life the beauty of Christ.

I bless Thee for those who serve in lonely places.

I bless Thee for the beautiful world in which I am allowed to live—for the freshness of the morning, the glory of the sun, the music of the wind; for trees and flowers, and the innumerable things of grass and garden that I pass almost unseen. I bless Thee for the strong ministries of human love —for the tie that binds men and women, the confidence of little children, the encouragement of friends.

I bless Thee for the stirring ministry of the past—for good men and women who have passed this way, some of whom are known to me by name.

Most of all, I bless Thee for those who through the years have brought to me by word of mouth, by the painter's art, and by the printer's craft, the unsearchable riches of Jesus Christ. Help me this day with humble heart to offer to Thee, and to those about me, a like service; for Jesu's sake. *Amen.*

EVENING PRAYER

Heavenly Father, I come to Thee at close of day with praise and thanksgiving on my lips.

I praise Thee that I have been allowed to live this day, and that from dawn till dusk, and into the darkness, Thy love remains constant about me.

In every age, men and women have heard the accents of Thy voice—in the mysterious sounds of the winds, the green fruitfulness of the earth, the majesty of the mountains. I thank Thee that these things are part of my life still.

I thank Thee that men and women have felt Thy greatness near in times of quiet reflection on Thy Word, in secret prayer, and in corporate worship; and that these things are part of my life still.

I thank Thee that in the tangle of human affairs, in the struggle of their highest selves amidst things depressing and difficult, men and women have learned to know Thy will. I am filled with wonder that I may know it, too.

I have been dull and foolish. I have sometimes been unwilling to know Thy nearness, or to do Thy will. Forgive me.

Teach me, I pray Thee, to render humble service, gladly and freely, in the place where Thou hast set me. Give me, I pray Thee, a sense of kinship with the saints and splendid people of every age. May my will be wholly Thine, until Thy will is done in earth, as in Heaven. *Amen.*

His Thanks

READING: Colossians 3¹⁵

I knew old Tom Morland well from the time he began to tackle the class in the little country Sunday-school. It wasn't a big class: there were only ten boys, if there had been more I don't know how old Tom would have managed. He was too gentle. No one in the whole valley was more surprised, of course, than the old man himself when he was asked to take them—they had no teacher, and unless somebody tried they would have no class.

Those ten boys seemed to have more youthful devilry packed into them than most. The first morning, the old man faced them with the story of the ten lepers healed by Christ, —a lesson that had cost him half a week of evenings in preparation. They began by asking if it was true.

Somehow the old man managed week after week to keep their interest. Ten years went by, and there are many Sundays in ten years.

He has gone now; he died last autumn. He got very frail toward the end, and had to leave the valley and live with his son up in town. The silver jubilee was held at the little valley church, but he couldn't go. The guest-speaker for that occasion was a distinguished Christian doctor. He wasn't eloquent, but his being there at all was the most eloquent witness of the jubilee. The whole burden of his brief talk was about a class of ten boys.

And how glad he must be now that he sat down and wrote a letter to one who was not there to hear his speech of thanks. For the jubilee was scarcely over when there was a familiar name in the obituaries.

I saw that letter. Old Tom showed it to me with wonder in his pale blue eyes. 'Bless the good Lord!' he kept saying, his frail old mind mixing things up a bit. 'True? Didn't I say it was true—that there were ten of them—and one of them came back to say his thanks!'

MORNING PRAYER

Lord God, great Giver of Life, as I enter upon the new day before me, my first act is to bring Thee my thanks for life.

Let not my sense of well-being blind me to my continual need of Thy presence this day. Let my service be gladly given; let my judgements be wise and kind; let my patience be quiet and steady. If I have to bear unexpected burdens, let me but lean more heavily upon Thy strength.

Bless me in my dealings with others—especially young people. Enable me to see their point of view and to rejoice in their strength, their eagerness, their honesty, their laughter.

Deliver them from all that is artificial, all that would lower their vision. Give them tasks to do, and strength to do them. Give them a fierce hatred of all that is unjust, of all that denies the precious rights of life to others. Give them a quickened sense of their inheritance in the things of the mind and spirit. Let them abound in thanksgiving. *Amen.*

EVENING PRAYER

O God, my Father, who dwellest beyond all darkness, I bless Thee that Thou hast fashioned me for everlasting companionship with Thyself. I cannot understand how such a wondrous thing can be; I only know that I have learned from Jesus to call Thee 'Father'. I bless Thee for the certainty that Thou hast made me, and all that is, for Thine own.

Forgive me that I have ever forgotten my high destiny. Forgive me that I have ever faltered in my service to the other members of the family on earth.

Forgive me that I have ever felt superiority because of the colour of my skin, or the social position of my family, or the tradition of my school, or the dignity of my place of worship. Forgive me that I have ever been unfriendly to any. Forgive me that I have ever taken of right the good things of life—without returning to offer my thanks.

Ere I sleep, for every favour
This day showed
By my God,
I will bless my Saviour.

O my Lord, what shall I render
To Thy name,
Still the same,
Merciful and tender? Amen.

A Saint in Shabby Black

READING: Hebrews 12$^{1\cdot 2}$

You will not find the name of Elizabeth Pilenko listed among the earth's saints. You must not expect to find her wearing a halo of heavenly radiance—a shabby black habit is all that marks her out.

Who is she? A wealthy young girl from a privileged land-owning family. A student at the Women's University of St Petersburg. But the years pass quickly. Now she is Mayor of her town. Now she is in Paris—her heart filled with strange triumphs and conflicting griefs. Now she is finding her way to a living faith. She is founding an Abbey, though clearly she is no ordinary Russian Orthodox religious. When onlookers find courage to question her about it, her answer is always the same: 'I must go my way. I am for the suffering people.'

Morning after morning she is in the market buying cheap food for the poor she feeds. The very poor, the Russian refugees without country, claim, or future, call her Mother Maria. In shabby black, but with eyes shining with purpose, she goes in and out. She has no time to think of herself. Her shabby black becomes more shabby, her shoes more worn.

Refugees suffering from tuberculosis are lying in a filthy hovel on the Seine bank with syphilitic wrecks that the police have picked up. She has no money in her shabby market-bag save a few francs. But she is rich—rich in the love that can work miracles for her Lord. She opens an old château for the poor wretches of the river-bank.

Time hastens on. Hitler's armies are surging in like a flood. Her roof is a shelter for hunted Jews, and for women and children. But time is running out. The Gestapo hammer at her door. They seem a little taken aback when they find that their prisoner is only a frail woman in shabby black. They do not understand a battle in which the only weapon is love. But the deed for which they have come must be done, and Mother Maria is hounded off with others to the concentration camp at Ravensbrueck.

As day follows day her hours are full. Two and a half years

of what seems timeless time pass by. She is older and shabbier now, and bearing the marks of pain. In the camp a new building is raised. The prisoners are told it will contain baths, but in time the awful truth dawns upon them. One morning there is an order, and a queue. Twenty women are lined up. One of the doomed twenty is a young girl who has become hysterical. A strong arm goes about her shoulder and turns her away. In her place is one who cannot now keep out of that queue.

And so, in line with the rest, clothed only in shabby black, a saint passes through the doors to death. It is Good Friday, 1945.

MORNING PRAYER

O Lord of self-forgetting Love, as I look out upon life and remember the debt I owe to many great souls who have passed this way, I bring Thee my adoration and praise that human love is capable of so much.

Hallow every moment of this day. Keep me, by Thy grace, free from all that is little and mean and unworthy. Let not the pressure of life with its countless claims, find me unready. Garrison my spirit with quietness and serene trust. Let my hands be ready to serve. Lift my eyes to where the everlasting things are clearly seen.

May there be nothing in this day of which I shall need to be ashamed when the sun is set, or at the end of the way when I come to my eternal Home and see Thy face. *Amen*.

EVENING PRAYER

Lord of my life and Father of my whole being, who dost give to me the very breath I breathe, and every power to move and think and feel, I thank Thee that Thou art always breaking in upon my days in new experiences, in new friends, in new responsibilities. Thou dost not despair of my poor powers, but dost use them, filling them out with Thy divine strength.

I bless Thee for all brave men and women. I bless Thee especially for all those who have shown me how life can be raised from the dust of earth to be a thing of everlasting worth.

Give Thy holy courage, this night, to all who suffer cruelty,

18

all who are crushed in spirit, all who are made to walk the way of shame.

I praise Thee for the triumph of Jesus, who, suffering the worst that men could do to Him, came forth whole and glorious. I praise Thee that He companies here and now with all who in their need, stretch out hands of faith. May His Spirit empower and sustain them.

And may Jesus live within me, and His rich joy walk beside me. I wait in faith to know His nearness—for the day is far spent. *Amen.*

In a Little Back Street

READING: Psalm 90¹⁷

She worked among the city's poor, so she had long known the back streets. A visitor like myself might be told that the great city was home to many thousands of people. She knew the homes of many of them. A visitor might be shown the great buildings and public parks. She knew parts of the city where a green tree had a struggle to grow. Some were near the railways with their soot and grime; some were by the docks.

Then an unforgettable day came. For the first time she found herself with a little house of her own. True, it was in a poor part of the city, but it was her own.

With a woman's eagerness she set her few things about her. She hemmed her curtains. She hung her pictures on the walls. She set out her cherished cups and saucers. She scrubbed her front doorstep, and polished her knocker. It was many a year since that old door-knocker had answered to the light of the sun with a glowing face.

The next task was with a little piece of sour earth between her doorstep and the street. Once, long ago, it had been a garden. Now she dug it and opened it to the warmth of the spring. She must make it into a lawn, she told herself, for she had never had a lawn.

Eagerly she went to the seed-merchant. 'I've served all my life among the poor of this old city,' she said, 'and now I've got a little place of my own. In front of it is a little piece of earth that I've dug and prepared. Now I must have some seed for it. And please, *can* I have the seed with the daisies in it?'

The seed with the daisies in it! The essential things we must have—the practical things. But, please God, let us have some daisies, too—extra things and beautiful. We cannot live without our daisies!

20

MORNING PRAYER

'Let not beauty die for me. May dawn and sunset, twilight and storm, hold their thrill to the last; may the young moon still cradle magic and the old moon image peace; may the wind never fail to blow freedom into my nostrils, and the sunlight strike to my heart till I die. And if colour, light, shadow and the sound of birds calling all fall from my failing senses, at least let the touch of earth be sweet to my fingers and the air to my eyelids.'

Draw especially near, I beseech Thee, to all who live in great cities, where bleak buildings and chimney-pots shut out the sky, and the children must play in the streets. Bless all who try, against odds, to bring beauty into homes and schools and places of work. Give patience and encouragement to all who serve in drab places, through the ministry of the Church.

Quicken within me today a new sense of social responsibility for the lives of the masses, who are not 'masses' to Thee, but men and women and little children—everlasting spirits, housed in bodies with a claim to consideration and care.

Let me not forget that in Jesus Thou hast shown Thy compassion for the multitudes, that 'a city drew Him', and that 'He wept' over a city.

In Thy mercy, draw near this day to all who look out upon life through dull or bitter eyes, especially all whose bodies are starved or stunted or broken, all whose spirits have failed to waken to the glory of living, whose minds have never found their way into that wide kingdom whose key is wonder.

Forgive me those things in my heart and mind which are still ugly and contrary to Thy kingdom. Many of them I have successfully hidden from my friends; but I cannot hide them from Thee. Have mercy upon me, and make me anew this day. *Amen.*

EVENING PRAYER

Gracious Father, I would pray especially for all with whom I have had dealings this day. Bless them as they come to their rest. Forgive them their failures, and forgive me wherein I have failed them, and Thee.

I ask a special blessing on all those who have resisted strong temptation this day; for all those who have chosen the way of the Lord Christ, not because they must, but with all the kingdoms of the earth in sight.

I pray especially for all whose work has been without interest this day, for all who have lacked creative satisfaction, for all whose work has been beyond their strength or skill, for all whose work has afforded them but a niggardly reward, and for all who have worked today in dangerous or ugly places.

Amen.

The Church of the Resurrection

READING: 1 Peter 1³

The quiet town did not know much of war. It had only one raid, but at the end of that twenty minutes four-fifths of its buildings, including every one of its five churches, were in ruins.

Some said Pforzheim would never recover from the blow. And it seemed they were right, for three and a half years later only one new building had been raised. But to a few people that new building was a sign. It was a little church that stood on a hill overlooking the devastated town. They called it 'The Church of the Resurrection'.

Coming together when all things material had been shattered, they had faced the prospect of long years without proper houses and food. But if they were to survive such a way of life, they knew that they must have a place where in quietness they could wait upon God.

That is why they made their way up the hill together and laid the foundations. Materials were few. The World Council of Churches helped; the young folk of the German *Hilfswerk* raised the frame; all worked on the walls with bricks from bombed houses.

Now those who gather for worship Sunday after Sunday do not forget the name of their church, 'The Church of the Resurrection'. Nor do they forget the quiet words on the first occasion when they gathered: 'There is not one of us but has sacrificed much,' said the speaker. 'But where two or three meet in the wilderness, and know one another, they remain together. And whether there be thirty or forty or four hundred, they build a community of silence, of hesitant words and of sudden prayer and singing. And such a community lays down a ring of stones and builds . . . not only to assure their being together, but also to make visible and real in life, their spiritual community, part of the living Body of Christ in the world.'

This they did—by faith—in Pforzheim. In the midst of death and most grievous loss the Resurrection became a present-day fact.

23

MORNING PRAYER

Eternal Father, reaching down to our earth in Jesus Christ, I thank Thee for the unimaginable powers of the Resurrection. I marvel that when all seemed lost and destroyed and utterly done away by hate, Thou didst bring the triumph of the world's first Easter morning.

I bless Thee for the women who went early to receive the incredible news. I bless Thee for those who put that news to every possible test, even the test of their own broken, dispirited lives. I rejoice greatly in the new power that sent them into all the world; I bless Thee for the triumphant reality made manifest in ten thousand, thousand lives. Grant that it may be the most real thing in my experience this day. Let others learn from me that Christ lives, that He lives for evermore. That He is eternally greater than my sin, that He is nearer than breathing and closer than hands or feet.

I bless Thee for Thy great Church in the world. Strengthen and revitalize her witness, that men and women everywhere may know the living Christ, and be lifted out of darkness and defeat and despair.

I pray for our sadly troubled world—for the nations, and the leaders of the nations; for all those whose designs are evil; for those who ferment national and social unrest, and will not know themselves part of the great family of God. Forbid that I should despise any for whom Christ went to the Cross, and the Tomb, or that I should do injury to any in whom His spirit lives. Hasten the day when the darkness of men's sin in war and destruction shall surrender to the dominion of the Prince of Peace, and to the power of His Resurrection. *Amen*.

EVENING PRAYER

Eternal Father who art ever near me, when I am fresh in the morning, and when I am weary at night, I bring Thee my adoration.

Forgive me wherein I have been forgetful of Thy high purpose, this day, wherein I have been lacking in love. Bless all the weary in body and mind, this night; and all the lonely. Bless all those who have no loved ones to welcome them in with understanding.

Have mercy on all who are bereaved or sorrowful. Have mercy on those who have brought needless suffering upon themselves and others.

Bless with thankful hearts those to whom this day has brought some special happiness. Bless with continuing wonder those who have fallen in love this day, those who have entered upon the mysteries of parenthood, those who have given their energies to the responsibilities of home-making.

Strengthen the ties that bind our hearts together in love and mutual care. Make us sensitive to the needs of others, that we may share gladly the good things of life.

Guide and bless with true vision those who preach and teach; all those who prepare the films of the people, and present the plays, and perform the music; those who write the books, and the papers and magazines that colour our minds. Grant skill and gentleness to all dedicated to the ministry of healing—doctors and nurses and orderlies and laboratory workers.

Wrap us around with Thy love, as the night enwraps the earth, and give us rest and renewal, that on the morrow we may serve Thee better; for Jesu's sake. *Amen.*

Of Him are All Things

READING: Romans 11³³⁻⁶, 12¹⁻²

Again I was in Sussex, walking over the Downs with a friend. Our talk was of many things dear to our hearts. And at East Dean we turned into the little church.

East Dean, set in gentle sheep-country, goes back to the beginnings of human settlement. On the hills encircling the village are lonely tumuli, great earthworks and lines of primitive field-culture. It was something as simple but of much more recent date, within the little church, that stirred my heart. There, set beautifully amid the things of Nature and men's toil, we found a crook—just an ordinary shepherd's crook. But beside it I read these words: 'This crook belonged to Richard Fowler of East Dean, who through a long life tended flocks of Southdown sheep. . . . His crook has a link with the Parish Church, East Dean, in that it once served a Bishop as his pastoral staff. The Bishop was Dr Walter Andrews. One summer evening in June 1929 he arrived to take a Confirmation, but without a pastoral staff. This omission was remedied by Richard Fowler, who was returning home with his crook and dog after folding his sheep under Bell Tout. . . . So one shepherd borrowed of another shepherd—and to the contentment of confirmees and congregation, the Bishop carried the crook.'

> There was a Man who dwelt
>   in the east centuries ago,
> And now I cannot look at a sheep,
>   or a sparrow,
> A lily or a cornfield, a raven
>   or a sunset,
> A vineyard or a mountain, without
>   thinking of Him;
> If this is not to be divine,
>   what is?

For long, religion was busy with divisions between 'secular' and 'sacred'. But Jesus refused to recognize any such division.

26

He loved, and offered to God's service, the commonplace things of every day.

At East Dean it was not difficult to remember that He called Himself *the Good Shepherd.*

MORNING PRAYER

O God my Father, in whom I live and move and have my being, Thy creative power and beauty is all around me in the world which Thou hast made. The morning sun rejoices at Thy bidding, and the trees grow and the mountains raise their heads on high. I bless Thee for the commonplace joys of hot water and good food, for the fellowship of kindred minds, for the satisfaction of work to do and strength to do it.

I bless Thee that Jesus Christ, Thy son, our Lord, walked this human way; that in His sight nothing that ministered to life was unworthy of the notice of God. Let me look at commonplace things through His eyes today, and carry His spirit into my work. Let me show courtesy and consideration to all other workers whom I shall meet, especially those who must travel on crowded buses or trains, or work in cold, dangerous, or drab places.

Where there is friction, let understanding be born; where there is domination, reverence for the worker. So let the looms and the wheels of commerce move to Thy praise; so let tedious and commonplace tasks be done to Thy glory, for the sake of Him who loved the common things of earth. *Amen.*

EVENING PRAYER

Gracious Lord, as the evening draws in and the noises of the busy day are hushed, I bless Thee for the responsibilities of this day. Thou hast blessed my going out and my coming in.

I bless Thee for the thousand interests of a commonplace day: for my home and for those who have come to depend upon me there; for my work and those who share it with me week in and week out; for my leisure and its gift of books and music, of chosen crafts, of gardening and walking and friendship.

I thank Thee that Thou hast set me to live in a world that is full of a thousand riches. I bless Thee for rhythm and colour and form, for human courage and tenderness, for self-forgetfulness and good fun. I thank Thee for those who are young and share the gifts of strength and eagerness, and for those who are old, whose wisdom has been enriched by the gathering of the years.

All my loved ones I commend to Thee, knowing well that they were Thine and were loved of Thee long before ever I fashioned a prayer for them.

Gather us in; we are Thy children. *Amen.*

Our Father

READING: Acts 17²²⁻⁸

The French army had retreated, but the little Waldensian village was still full of men—two hundred of them. They were sick and wounded, and the village people took them into their homes and did what they could for them.

The village people had always been poor, and now they were made poorer still by war. None of the wounded could work, and few could walk. They were men of France, enemies against whom the people of Bobbi had fought bitterly.

Days passed into weeks, and summer drew to a close. Still no word came as to what was to be done with the men. They did not even worship in the same way, but the villagers sought out their old pastor. 'What is to be done?' they asked. 'These men have need of food and compassion that we are poorly able to give. What little we have must go to our children, and the aged of the village.'

'I do not know,' replied the old pastor. 'But always when I do not know what to do, I pray. Call together the village and we will ask God what He wants us to do.'

And it was so. Those of simple Christian faith gathered and, led by their pastor, sought the will of God. 'Show us,' they prayed, 'how to help these men from beyond the mountains.'

As they rose from their knees, one man said: 'As we prayed, I knew there was something I could do. I will offer God my strength to carry one man over the Col de Croix.' Said another: 'I also will offer God my strength. Freed of the weight of their packs, many of the men could walk.'

But the Col de Croix was a high and dangerous pass. Eternal snows lay there. To make the crossing would be difficult even for men of the mountains. But their hearts were set upon it. And on a day in autumn they started out with the men whom they might have killed in battle.

There were times in that terrible crossing when it seemed they might have to turn back. But at last they made their way down into the French village, and restored the sick and wounded to their wives and families.

29

As—their task done—they turned to make their way back over the pass, the cheering villagers bade them God-speed.

'Their gratitude is plain,' said one of the men. 'This is a great thing we have done.'

But the old pastor, who had shared in the hazards of the journey, answered: 'Nay, Nay. Spare us such words. It is not great. It is only Christian. In this act of brotherhood we have but earned the right to call the God of all men "Our Father".'

MORNING PRAYER

Loving Father, amidst the comfort of my days, I remember before Thee those who suffer, those separated from their loved ones, those who bear the grim and costly burden of war, those who are disabled in body and mind, those who are lonely, and those without anyone to turn to in their distress.

Thou hast made us to be one family upon the earth. Help me not only to receive the unearned good that comes because I belong to the family, but also to share the family responsibilities. Give me a quickened imagination that I may understand how things seem to others; make me generous in sympathy, and instant in service. In good works let not my left hand know what my right hand doeth; let me serve for Thy sake, and because I take upon my lips daily the words of the family prayer:

'*Our* Father, which art in heaven,
Hallowed be Thy name.
Thy kingdom come.
Thy will be done in earth, as it is in heaven.
Give us this day our daily bread.
And forgive us our trespasses, as we forgive them that trespass against us.
And lead us not into temptation; but deliver us from evil: For Thine is the kingdom, the power, and the glory, for ever and ever. *Amen.*'

EVENING PRAYER

Gracious Father, I bless Thee for the precious gift of night. At Thy feet I lay the service of this day. Thou knowest the brave purposes of the morning that have not been fulfilled. Thou knowest the temptations Thou hast enabled me to overcome this day. Thou knowest the service that I have been allowed to do. Thou knowest my inmost thoughts as they are known to no other. And Thou knowest that I love Thee. Help me to love Thee more worthily.

I thank Thee for the many who have loved Thee; for their courage in times of difficulty, for their gaiety of heart, for their generous self-giving. I bless Thee for the loving service of those who speak a language different from my own and follow a way of life that is strange to me. I thank Thee for good home-loving people, and for every hand out-stretched to help another on the way.

I bless Thee for the great ministry of the Church in all the world, and in my own part of the world. Strengthen her witness in these challenging days, that men and women, Thy children, may learn how to live, and find their way Home.

And now, with the gift of Thy forgiveness, grant me Thy peace, and quiet sleep. *Amen.*

She Had No Halo

READING: 1 Corinthians 13¹⁻¹³

I made my way up to Liverpool. I wanted to see the great Cathedral, built in this century and still echoing the sound of the mason's hammer. But most of all I wanted to see its Lady Chapel, with its window to the memory of Kitty Wilkinson.

In many another place of worship the craftsman's lovely colours—blue of the sky, green of the earth, gold of the sun, and blood-red like the most precious gift poured out—have been assembled to depict the saints in their haloes and the heroes with their flaming swords. But how few windows there are to people like Kitty Wilkinson.

In a mean street stood her little house, its door open to all who came—the ill-clad, the unloved, the unhappy, the aged. And when the dread cholera struck the city, Kitty scarcely rested night or day. Many died, and the street where Kitty's house stood was badly stricken. From house to house she went, nursing the sick, bringing comfort where death had entered, doing all she could to combat the dread disease.

Kitty Wilkinson was a woman of practical sense; she saw how little good it was only to preach wisdom—she practised it.

She was not slow to realize that lack of pure water and proper washing facilities encouraged the spread of the epidemic. The city supply was often cut off; but Kitty had a well. And to her well and tiny kitchen came as many as seventy families a week to do their washing.

The importance of water and public cleanliness gradually came to be realized by the authorities. And they raised in the city of Liverpool the first public baths and wash-houses for the poor. Very fittingly, Kitty and her husband Tom were appointed caretakers.

It was a wonderful thing. Countless poor families blessed God for Kitty Wilkinson, as her epitaph shows: 'Indefatigable and self-sacrificing, she was the widow's friend, the support of the orphan, the fearless and unwearied nurse of the sick, the originator of baths and wash-houses of the poor.'

So Kitty Wilkinson has her place secure in the gratitude of the nation, and her stained-glass window among the saints —the Saint of the Soap-suds.

MORNING PRAYER

Gracious Father, turn my hands to practical service this day, that I may add something to the world. Let not my eyes be only toward distant places, so that I miss the opportunity for service close at hand. Give me a lively concern for those whose lives are burdened by want, sickness, or ignorance. Let loving-kindness be the mark of all my service, and patient knowledge and courage.

I ask Thy blessing this day on all who work to lighten the lot of those in great cities, for social-workers and deaconesses and nurses, for those who administer justice, for directors of business and those whom they employ, and for all who keep the streets clean, the water pure, and our homes safe.

Bless all those who help to fashion the city's thought— those who prepare its daily newspapers, present its films and plays, and perform its music. Bless those who preach in its churches and lead the people in service. Bless all who teach in schools and colleges; and those who help to develop the bodies, minds and spirits of youth. Bless all who prepare good meals, and who keep open door and open heart to those with special need.

In my comings and goings today, let me serve Thee, through faithfulness in the place where Thou hast set me; for Jesu's sake, who took the servant's bowl, and washed the disciples' feet. *Amen.*

EVENING PRAYER

O Lord our Creator and Redeemer, I bless Thee that Thou hast made us dependent upon each other for the needs of our bodies, the stimulus of our minds, and the quickening of our spirits.

But I bless Thee also for moments of solitude—when I can think upon the things of life, alone in Thy presence; and for the many decisions that I must make for myself—not depending upon the wisdom and good spirit of others.

I bless Thee for books, and for leisure, often dearly bought, in which to enjoy them; for music which others have made for me; and for the natural delight of human fellowship—for conversation, and mutual trust.

I bless Thee most of all for my personal relationship with Jesus Christ, my Lord and Saviour, so that at the day's end—as in every other part of it—I can look up into Thy face, and know Thy loving strength about me, forgiving and restoring and blessing me. Thou hast set eternity in my heart, so that no earthly thing, however good, can satisfy me wholly. In quietness and confidence, I rejoice in this knowledge, and take the gift of rest. Of Thy love and Thy strength and Thy greatness, there is no end. *Amen.*

The Eternal Hope

READING: 1 Corinthians 15[19-22]

The 'man who loved the world' was dead.

Klaas Havenga, his old and formidable opponent, called him that. Speaking of Jan Smuts, he said: 'He rose from height to height, and his light was spread far beyond the bounds of his course . . . his country was the world, and I had to be content with the more particular sphere of South Africa.'

Yet during the whole of his eighty years, how dearly he loved South Africa! Born on a Cape farm, he was familiar from earliest days with the sights and scents and sounds of the African scene.

In time, he found his way to Stellenbosch. He was the most brilliant student of his year, and a scholarship took him to Cambridge, where the many qualities of his fine mind were turned toward the study of Law. In time he was called to the Bar.

Then South Africa—the country of the sights and scents and sounds he knew, and of the wide spaces, and wakening human passions—drew him back. And he returned to practise as an advocate at the Cape—to fall in love with Table Mountain, and with a childhood friend and fellow-student.

How well she stood by him in the strange, changeful years of public life that lay ahead! Peace and war, and political struggle and misunderstanding were all part of those years. But all the time there was 'Isie', growing grey in the service of truth. In the Second World War, the Springbok soldiers, whom she served devotedly, were to christen her *Ouma* (Grannie). And all the time there was Table Mountain, where he could climb to escape the wordy battles of men.

When his death was known, the proud city of Pretoria, was silent. It was a city of sorrow and mourning for Jan Christiaan Smuts. His last trek was over. Across the veld rode a white-bearded company of *oudstryders*, his old comrades-in-arms, determined to go as far with him on the last trek as they might.

The crowds that gathered outside the plain and dignified

35

Groote Kerk were as silent as those within. They too had come as far as they might with their old leader or their old opponent. Ouma, however, was not present. She had elected to remain silently at the old farm-home, *Doornkloof*, that they had made together. But her flowers were on his coffin —the red, purple and white heather of the Cape, their birthplace, where sixty-odd years ago they had fallen in love. And on those simple flowers there was a card, and on it her last message: '*Tot siens, Pappa*'—See you soon, Pappa.

MORNING PRAYER

O Lord of Sincerity and Truth, before whom all that is hollow and unreal is consumed away, give me the spirit of reality. Thou who art the Light and the Life of all who journey by this human way, make me to know Thy presence when I cannot be sure of the presence of any other.

Thou hast taken the sting from death and the darkness from the grave, through the Resurrection of Jesus Christ. Thou hast lifted up the eyes of all who follow in His way, to see beyond the things which are here and now, to that life which is everlasting. Unto Thee be all glory, might, majesty, dominion and power, now and for evermore.

Into Thy holy and loving keeping I commend all those who are dear to me. Thou hast tied together our human hearts and lives; draw especially near when the time comes for us to part. Give us, when we come to the end of the day, only gratitude for the experience of life and quiet trust. We have heard the strong, comforting word of Jesus, and we know that because He lives, we too shall live. Give us courage to go on in faith until the morning breaks, and we are united once more.
Amen.

EVENING PRAYER

Eternal God, our Father, we would worship Thee not only when life's sun is high and our burdens are gladly borne, but when our heads are bowed. Help us in the day of parting to take our leave of those who are dear to us in quietness and confidence. Let us not sorrow as those without hope, but sustain us by the knowledge of Thy Eternal goodness; for we are 'persuaded that neither death nor life, nor angels nor principalities nor powers, nor things present, nor things to come, nor height nor depth, nor any other creature shall be able to separate us from the love of God, which is in Christ Jesus, our Lord'. *Amen.*

The Sure Foundation

READING: 1 Corinthians 3⁹⁻¹¹

For a thousand years men have walked and worshipped in Winchester. Indeed, one of the earliest churches was built there, and descriptions of it have come down from the days of Lucius the Roman. His church was utterly destroyed, though persecution could not annihilate the Christians. Then the church was re-built by the Saxons; then again razed to the ground. But the purpose of Walkelyn, kinsman of the Conqueror, was to build more gloriously. Tradition says that he asked for its building all the oak that could be felled from Hempage Wood in four days and nights, and, when the King had given consent, set an army to work and removed the whole wood.

William of Wykeham, in his turn, transformed the edifice, raised it, and with superb craftsmanship gave it the magnificence that it bears today.

But it was left to two men of this century to do for Winchester the most surprising service. News that the great church was sinking brought Sir Francis Fox hastening to Winchester. In parts the church had sunk two feet. Some of its arches were distorted, and great cracks were visible.

Sir Francis dug down by the south wall and made a discovery. Eight feet down the masonry stopped. Then the ancient tale of the oaken logs came to his mind. Laid on the peat bog, like a great raft, they had served for eight hundred years. But their work at last was done. They were no foundation now for this precious medieval shrine, and it seemed certain that catastrophe awaited it.

Then Sir Francis called in a diver, William Walker. Together they saved Winchester. It took five years after the fabric had been cleaned and scaffolded and strengthened. For all those five years William Walker grovelled under the great Cathedral. The peaty water was so black that no light could penetrate it. He brought up peat, a handful at a time. And in its stead he laid bags of concrete. In the dark he laid four layers. Then concrete blocks were sunk, and the pumping

38

out of the water was begun. From pit to pit William Walker made his way till, with his own hands, he had laid a completely new foundation under the ancient building.

It is little wonder that William Walker had his place beside their Majesties the King and Queen when in 1912 they attended a great service of thanksgiving in Winchester Cathedral. And it is little wonder that there was much talk about foundations that day.

MORNING PRAYER

Eternal Father, I thank Thee for all who have raised gracious buildings wherein men have assembled to worship for centuries, and for all honest craftsmen who today delight to work for Thy Church.

I bless Thee for all who have a deep concern for the foundations of the State, the school, and the home, who serve Thee and their fellow-men with joy, and in whose building shoddy work has no place.

I bless Thee for all who within the Church, have set their faith firmly on the foundation of Jesus Christ. Make me wise enough to reject every other foundation, and brave enough to reject any superstructure unworthy of the great Foundation. Let me bring to the adornment of my faith gifts of mind and artistic judgement. Let me choose well the convictions that find a lodging place in my soul; let me value beyond price the ministry of quiet and prayer. Let Thy beauty, Lord my God, be upon me, and in all that I do, or say, direct my energies; for Jesu's sake. *Amen.*

EVENING PRAYER

O Thou who dwellest where night never comes, draw near to me now as darkness moves over the earth. Forgive my stumbling words. Speak to me in Thine own good way.

From olden times men and women have turned from the clamour of life to hear Thy voice, forgiving, guiding and directing; and I would hear it now. Hear me speedily, O Lord. Cause me to hear.

In Thy presence let all that is hollow and unreal be consumed away. Make me brave enough to bear the truth. Make me in this hour aware of my own frailties, and give me a greater dependence upon Thee.

O Lord, how near Thou art! How great! How dependable! How loving!

> All-loving—but Thy love is stern
>   And claims, not love alone, but deeds:
> It profits little if I burn
>   With rapture, while my brother bleeds;
> Further my love with practical intent,
> Lest it evaporate in sentiment.
>   Amen.

Can the Blind Lead?

READING: Mark 8¹⁸

A fragment of one of the Master's questions was in my mind as I walked about the great city that spring morning.

'With your love of books,' said my blind friend, 'you ought to step into the Braille Library.'

I assured him I would. Two mornings later I made my way there. I was greeted by the middle-aged librarian. Very graciously she came round from behind her counter. 'We have most of your books here,' she said. 'Would you like to see one of them in Braille?'

Instantly I felt a great care not to embarrass her. I felt sure that she had mistaken my name. 'I will have one of them brought,' she continued. 'Which one would you like?'

Thinking still to save her, I replied: 'Oh, you choose!'

Presently the volumes came—three large ones equivalent to one ordinary volume.

'Would you like me to read something from one of them?' she asked. 'What would you like?'

But it was my turn now to feel that I lacked sight—or, that I lacked insight. I could not tell if indeed it was a book of mine that she held; or if it was, which one it was; or which passage she would choose to read back to me. And I cannot easily tell of my emotion when that spring morning she read to me something of my joy in the spring I had written years before.

Thinking of the fourteen million partially or totally blind, Helen Keller said: 'Blindness is to live immured, baffled, all God's world of colour shut out. It is to sit helpless, staring into the dark, with nothing but the dark staring back, whilst one's spirit tugs at the fetters.' But when asked if there were not a greater misfortune, she added, unforgettably: 'Yes—it is to have eyesight, and not to be able to see!'

MORNING PRAYER

O God, my Father, the heavens declare Thy glory, and the firmament showeth Thy handiwork. The night sky with its myriad stars speaks of Thy steadfastness, and the new day calls to renewed dedication to Thy purpose.

I bless Thee for the miracle of the seasons, each with its colour and form, each with its part in the endless pattern of Time. I bless Thee especially for the spring, the birthday of the year, for its gaiety and hope. I bless Thee for bursting buds and changeful skies, for tender colour and form. I bless Thee for senses to apprehend this glorious gift, especially for eyes to trace its youthful loveliness.

Forgive me if I have been unresponsive, if I have allowed even the tiny things to remain unseen. Forgive me if I have not praised Thee for the great gift of sight.

Draw especially near to all from whom the delights of the eye are withheld. Give them great patience as they grope their way in the darkness; give them compensating joys, and insight into the more lasting beauties of life. Especially let Thy blessing fall on those bereft of sight at the end of years; give them the power to recall the many colours and forms of life which they have enjoyed.

Make us all more and more aware of Thy beauties in the world that is visible, and in the world of mind and spirit, that we may together rejoice in Thy goodness through all our days.

Amen.

EVENING PRAYER

O Lord, Thou hast searched me and known me.

Thou knowest my downsitting and mine uprising, Thou understandest my thought afar off.

Thou compassest my path and my lying down, and art acquainted with all my ways.

For there is not a word in my tongue, but lo, O Lord, Thou knowest it altogether.

Thou hast beset me behind and before and laid Thine hand upon me.

Such knowledge is too wonderful for me; it is high, I cannot attain unto it.

Whither shall I go from Thy spirit, or whither shall I flee from Thy presence?

If I ascend up into heaven, Thou art there: if I make my bed in hell, behold, Thou art there.

If I take the wings of the morning, and dwell in the uttermost parts of the sea;

Even there shall Thy hand lead me, and Thy right hand shall hold me.

If I say, Surely the darkness shall cover me, even the night shall be light about me.

Yea, the darkness hideth not from Thee; but the night shineth as the day: the darkness and the light are both alike to Thee.

How precious also are Thy thoughts unto me, O God; how great is the sum of them!

If I should count them, they are more in number than the sand: when I awake, I am still with Thee.

Search me, O God, and know my heart; try me, and know my thoughts;

And see if there be any wicked way in me, and lead me in the way everlasting. *Amen.*

The Utmost for the Highest

READING: Romans 12$^{1-2}$

To the doctor and his wife on the wild borders of the Khyber Hills danger was as daily bread. But they had never asked for less. On one thing they were agreed—if the service of God was worth anything, it was worth everything.

There came a day in 1923 when a persistent knocking at the door was heard. Dr Harold Starr opened it expecting to see a patient. Instead it was a fanatic from the hills, who lifted a knife there and then and killed the Doctor on his own doorstep.

The doctor's wife had always known of the wild men in that hilly country between India and Afghanistan. Now she understood their need more deeply than ever.

To assuage her grief, she would go back to England to train, and would return to carry on as she could the doctor's work; and she would serve with her life the very tribe of his murderer.

Once more from the hills men descended with vengeance in their hearts. They fell this time on the home of Major Ellis at Kohat. They struggled with the Major, murdered his wife, and carried off his daughter.

For days there was no knowing the young girl's fate, but the doctor's widow felt she ought to do something about it.

The tribesmen were quick to warn her against interfering. But her mind was made up; she would find the girl if already she had not shared her mother's fate.

At last Mrs Starr came face to face with the tribesman who had done the murder. For hours they parleyed. And when it seemed that she had gained her point, she was herself suddenly seized. Then events took a rapid change. To Mrs Starr's surprise, the tribal priest rose up and solemnly cursed the murderer in the name of his religion.

And whilst the mood of the tribe was thus temporarily changed, the doctor's widow seized the girl for whom she had hazarded so much, and they made their escape.

In time, the news got out to the larger world. The King conferred on her the Kaiser-i-Hind Gold Medal for Public

44

Services in India, and the Order of St John of Jerusalem inscribed her name on the Tablet of Honour. But the doctor's widow lived in those dangerous parts to save life, and to her it seemed scarcely to matter whether she did it in one way or another. *If the service of God was worth anything, it was worth everything.*

MORNING PRAYER

O Lord of All, in whose hands are the issues of life and death, Thou hast taught me to do Thy will in the world. Enable me today to pray, 'Thy will be done, Thy Kingdom come', with the consent of all my faculties. I bring Thee my will at the beginning of this day, that it may be truly Thine.

> *Laid on Thine altar, O my Lord divine,*
> *Accept this gift today, for Jesu's sake:*
> *I have no jewels to adorn Thy shrine,*
> *No far-famed sacrifice to make;*
> *But here within my trembling hand I bring*
> *This will of mine—a thing that seemeth small,*
> *But Thou alone, O Lord, canst understand*
> *How when I yield Thee this, I yield mine all.*
> *Amen.*

EVENING PRAYER

Heavenly Father, I marvel that whether I sleep or wake, live or die, I am Thine.

I bless Thee for all who have enjoyed with me this day the privilege of life; for all who have consciously laid their wills upon Thine altar, knowing well that if Thy service is worth anything, it is worth everything. I bless Thee this night for all those whose service has been rendered in dangerous places. I bless Thee for the selfless ministry of missionary doctors. I bless Thee for all who have in any way made known Thy will to native and primitive peoples. I bless Thee for all who have planted seeds of peace and understanding in the place of cruelty and distrust. I pray for all who in the larger affairs of the nations have given unstinted service of body, mind and spirit, that peace may be established.

I pray for all who live in fear, for all who suffer at the hands of their fellows, for all whose days are saddened by family loss.

Give to all who must make important decisions a clear sense of Thy will. And to all of us grant Thy mercy without which we cannot live, or lie down in peace this night, or at the end. As the quiet stars look down upon the darkened world, do Thou look down upon our little lives, lifting us up into a clearer understanding of Thy great and loving purpose for us all.

'Teach us, good Lord, to serve Thee as Thou deservest; to give and not to count the cost; to fight and not to heed the wounds; to toil and not to seek for rest; to labour and not to ask for any reward, save that of knowing that we do Thy will; through Jesus Christ our Lord.' *Amen.*

The World Waits

READING: Ezekiel 9¹⁻²

That hour with the grey-haired man went like the wind over the hills. His grubby little back-street workshop must be one of the most romantic spots in the city. He was talking to me about brewing ink—yes, brewing.

Ink, I knew, had been made for thousands of years by the Egyptians. At first they inscribed their thoughts on stone, but later found that papyrus, a plant growing in the valley of the Nile, made a good substance on which to write.

'Of course, it was a big step forward when we got aniline,' said my ink-man. 'It has six carbon atoms, seven hydrogen and one nitrogen.' But I was not interested in formulas —it was the far-reaching possibilities of ink that held my imagination. We moved to one end of the workshop where drums of dye were standing. The contents of one looked like little coppery crystals. I took some into my hand as we stood talking. My hand was hot, and perhaps moist, and soon I had an inky blue hand. 'I thought you were taking a risk,' said my companion, 'but it will come off.' We looked at other drums—a blue-black, powdery one, and a full, fine red. He explained the process—a very simple one—and we moved to where the finished ink was being syphoned into two-ounce bottles. I saw the corks go in, and a little motor start up to help with the sticking on of the labels.

'Do you ever let your imagination loose whilst you are filling up these bottles ?' I asked. 'Do you wonder where they will all go, and what your ink will be used for ?'

Some will almost certainly be used to initiate little children into a wide and wonderful world, some for love-letters, some for business or friendly correspondence, some for the mundane task of keeping accounts, some perhaps for writing books, some even for anonymous letters—though that is an unworthy use.

'Yes; I think about it sometimes,' replied my old ink-man after a pause. 'First the thought, and then the ink, and then— who can tell ?'

So it comes about that lives are changed, reformations are made, slow plodding people are encouraged—and the glory of God breaks in upon us! Luther once threw a bottle of ink at the Devil. Today the world waits for young people with literary gifts, and with Christian minds and spirits, to throw a bottle of ink at all that is ugly and devilish in life.

MORNING PRAYER

O God, who hast wrought the world with exceeding beauty, let there be nothing in my life this day that will mar that beauty. The laws of Nature and the longings of my own heart proclaim Thee. Let me seek out Thy will, and do it. Let me follow after Thy truth, and love it.

In this quiet moment, call me back to my best self.

Let me show reverence this day for the bodies and minds and spirits of those with whom I have to do. Deliver me from the greed that seeks gain without labour, or the thrill of excitement without care for its cost to others. Deliver me this day from prejudice and intolerance and sentimentality, from all laziness that contents itself with half-truths, and arrogance that thinks it knows all truth. Wherever I can, in Thy strength, enable me to replace ugliness with beauty, evil with good, half-truths with Thy shining truth.

Bless especially today, all those who set down their thoughts and opinions for others—letter-writers, teachers of little children, leaders of youth, editors of newspapers and journals and those who work with them, authors and poets.

Let me hear again Thy question: 'What is that in thine hand?' And if it is a pen—let me use it to Thine honour and glory. *Amen.*

EVENING PRAYER

Eternal Father, who hast given me all things richly to enjoy, I bless Thee for neighbourly consideration, friendly conversation, and the laughter of little children. I praise Thee for honest men and women who have served gladly this day without fuss or thought of reward. I bring Thee my thanks for the gifts of science and invention that have added dignity to life, for the contribution of craftsmen and poets and painters; especially do I bless Thee for my favourite books and journals, and for all authors who have dedicated to Thee their gifts of mind and intellect, their powers of imagination and expression, of sympathy, common sense, and humour. For every glimpse of beauty I bless Thee, for every new truth that has beckoned me out beyond the place I have trod so often, or the opinion I have held so long.

I would respond to Thy love in my silence and in my speech, in my work and in my leisure, in the freshness of the morning and in the weariness of the evening, in company and in solitude.

Make me now certain of Thy forgiveness, and sensitive to Thy nearness. For the sake of my Saviour and Lord, Jesus Christ, give me a quiet mind. *Amen.*

Lest Lovely Things be Lost

READING: Psalm 119⁵⁴

Some said he was born into the wrong century—he should have been a minstrel. Others shook their heads and had no words when he threw over important legal work to play an organ in a cathedral. And the passage of time carried the rumour that he was conducting a choral society and presiding over an academy. It seemed to some a sad waste of gifts. When he kept turning up here and there as a musical tramp, it was well that they were not there to pass judgement. When he might have been hearing a *prima donna* in London, he was sitting with road-menders in ditches, and old grannies in cottage doorways, listening to their thin, cracked voices. From village to village he made his way, winning the shy confidence of the old and the poor. But he refused to call anyone poor who had a song in his heart.

It was not a good life for one with a tendency to asthma— and it was unpaid. But Cecil Sharp rejoiced in folk-songs, in their simple words and uncomplicated tunes.

In other countries—Germany, Russia, Austria—collections had been made; he would collect the songs of England. For he loved his England—her flowering ways, her village greens. He loved her simple labouring people who were the custodians of lovely things. 'He were an understandin' gentleman, he were,' said one old fellow. 'He had a powerful likin' for them old things. And I should say he were a good man, now.'

Even at the end of his life, Cecil Sharp could not tell how a folk-song came into being. Perhaps it was started by one happy spirit to tell of his love in the spring or of joy in his labour. Perhaps the next to sing it left out what he chose and added a line of his own, and at last something so tuneful and satisfying was made that it was altered no more.

All up and down the land Cecil Sharp made his way, seeking only one reward, till he laid down his frail body in death on a summer day. By that time he had gathered from the highways and byways the words and music of five thousand folk-songs.

Now nobody thinks Cecil Sharp born into the wrong century—they thank God that he was born into the twentieth century. For without him, many lovely things would have been lost.

MORNING PRAYER

> *My God, I thank Thee who hast made*
> *The earth so bright;*
> *So full of splendour and of joy,*
> *Beauty and light;*
> *So many glorious things are here,*
> *Noble and right!*
>
> *I thank Thee, too, that Thou hast made*
> *Joy to abound;*
> *So many gentle thoughts and deeds*
> *Circling us round,*
> *That in the darkest spot of earth,*
> *Some love is found.*

Gracious Lord, Thou hast given to me a rich heritage. I bless Thee for all good men and women who have passed this way, and have left some brightness or beauty for me to receive as my own. I thank Thee for all who have discovered songs or created them, lifting the burdens of this earthly way. I thank Thee for all who have served without thought of personal glory or gain. I pray that something of their rich spirit may be mine, that when I have gone my way, others may rejoice in something added to the world.

Bless all who teach little children to sing; bless all who make it easier for hard-working people to believe in beauty. Bless all who give of the rich things of life, without stint.

Let the place where I work, and the people amongst whom I work, be enriched by my serving this day; for the sake of Jesus the Man of Joy. *Amen.*

EVENING PRAYER

Father, the source of all good gifts, forgive me if this day I have been unresponsive to the beauty and music of Thy world.

Forgive me, if I have not rejoiced in the rising of the sun and the gladness of the morning, if I have not been grateful for the blood in my veins and the strength in my limbs. Forgive me if I have not answered to the call of my highest nature.

This night I bless Thee, forgetting not all Thy benefits:

that Thou forgivest all mine iniquities;

that Thou healest all my diseases;

that Thou redeemest my life from destruction;

that Thou crownest me with loving-kindness and tender mercies;

that Thou satisfiest my mouth with good things;

so that my youth is renewed like the eagle's.

If today I have been able to add some beauty to the world, or to restore some beauty that was lost, I bless Thee for that opportunity; if today I have been able to appreciate those who add beauty to the world, I bless Thee for that power.

In the comings and goings of my life, let the 'beauty of the Lord my God' be upon me. Never let me forget my high destiny, that one day I shall see the King in His beauty, and the land of far distances. *Amen.*

The Dusty Feet

READING: Matthew 20²⁷⁻⁸

I had scarcely drawn up my chair to the glow of the fire, when a little voice beside me said: 'Tell me the story of the dusty feet.'

I hesitated. The dusty feet? Could I make the story of the dusty feet understandable to a little child? I doubted whether I fully understood it myself. I remembered that someone had called it, 'The Sacrament of the Towel and Basin'.

I told about the house and the stairs, the lighted room at the top, the table set for the simple meal. I told about the friends gathered from the shadowy narrow streets of the city, whispering as they came, wondering who would be greatest. I told how they took their places in the softly lighted room. Then, I added, there was a pause. For any one of them to stoop to the lowly task of foot-washing was to proclaim himself servant of all, and that each was resolved he would never be.

Those friends were in no mood for their Master's words. Something had to be done—heated passions cooled, hearts made humble, and love quickened. But how? The answer was the 'story of the dusty feet'.

I saw again the bending figure of the Master; I heard again His words: 'He who would be greatest, let him be servant of all.'

And when the little one, her story done, had gone off to bed, I found it a steadying thought that our world has never quite lacked those who have shown such a spirit in the common affairs of life. Down the highway of humility God still comes to human hearts. When Dean Inge was in America, he stayed with the Quaker saint, Dr Rufus Jones. When bedtime came, the Dean, as his custom was, put his shoes outside his door. His host saw them, and in the morning they were cleaned. Morning after morning the simple service was repeated.

When Dean Inge was leaving, he said: 'Oh, Mr Jones, I've forgotten something. Will you give this dollar to the boy who cleaned my shoes?'

'Surely,' said his host, lest his guest should be discomforted.

Rufus Jones later told of the incident with a smile. It did not occur to that great soul that it revealed the spirit of Him who, long ago, poured water into a servant's basin, and washed the dusty feet.

MORNING PRAYER

O Lord of all those whose feet must travel this world's dusty ways, let me be master of myself this day, that I may be servant of others. Deliver me from all self-importance and from all pretence. Teach me the lasting secret of humility.

> *Lord make me an instrument of Thy peace.*
> *Where there is hatred, let me sow love;*
> *Where there is injury, pardon;*
> *Where there is doubt, faith;*
> *Where there is despair, hope;*
> *Where there is darkness, light;*
> *Where there is sadness, joy.*

O divine Master, grant that I may not so much seek to be consoled, as to console, to be understood as to understand, to be loved as to love. For it is in giving that we receive; it is in pardoning that we are pardoned; it is in dying that we are born to eternal life. *Amen.*

EVENING PRAYER

O Lord, who art Master of the night as of the day, who didst call the sleep from my eyelids and send me out, and who wouldst now gather me in to the quiet gentleness of sleep, I bless Thee for Thy mercy new every morning, and for Thy forgiveness sure every evening.

I pray for all those who have toiled this day, for all who have found satisfaction, and for those who have known disappointment and despair. I pray for all who have added their laughter to this day's life, for all who have set the lights dancing in the eyes of little children, for those who have set colour and

54

beauty in drab places. I bless Thee especially for those who have been an unconscious reminder of the humility of the Upper Room, for all who have washed the world's dusty feet this day.

In Thy mercy, forgive me that I have shown so little of that spirit in my dealings. So often pride has stood in the way, as in the Upper Room. Forgive me if today I have been filled with my own importance, if I have kept in my heart a grievance against another, if I have been eager for the punishment of any, and slow to seek his redemption. Forgive me if I have wasted my time or misused my gifts, if I have been unwilling to learn a new truth or to stoop to a lowly service.

Have mercy upon me according to Thy loving-kindness; according to the multitude of Thy tender mercies blot out all my transgressions. Wash me thoroughly from mine iniquity and cleanse me from my sin. Create in me a clean heart and renew a right spirit within me. *Amen.*

One Passion Planted Deep

READING: Psalm 8⁴⁻⁵

When Romany was not preaching, lecturing or broadcasting, he sought the woods and wild places. There was gipsy blood in his veins. The tiniest of furred and feathered things were assured of a place in his heart. For hours, in silence, he looked and listened, his old dog Raq beside him.

Always at the back of his experience was that day at Monkhill when he came upon a wild duck's nest. Within it were fourteen pale-green eggs. And the old desire awakened to push back yet farther the bounds of knowledge, that God's wild things might be better understood and loved. He stooped and picked up four of the eggs. How long he stood looking at them he could never remember.

On his way home Romany stopped, as he had promised, to lead the week-night worship of a handful of village people. The great things of God always held his wonder, and he was in the vestry before he thought again of the four green eggs in his pocket.

Fortunately no harm befell them, and at the end of weeks, four little ducklings were hatched out to an old mother hen. She managed well for a time, and saw no oddness in her lot; but when her little charges took to a tub of water at the end of the garden, some perplexity rose in her mothering heart.

Then came the night that Romany would never forget. He stood at the end of the garden watching the first pink strands of sunset cloud. The sky was beautiful, and over all was a great silence.

Then suddenly a cry reached his ears. He raised his eyes. Overhead a flight of wild duck, creatures of the great spaces, was speeding homewards.

The cry came again. And as suddenly three of the four young creatures that had sported happily in his restricted garden were up in the sky. The call of their God-given nature had reached them—they belonged to a larger life.

And when they had gone, Romany stood bare-headed and silent a long time. The colour died out of the sky, but some living words of St Augustine's were in his heart—and they remained there ever afterwards: 'Thou hast made us for Thyself, O God, and our heart is restless until it find its rest in Thee.'

MORNING PRAYER

Almighty God, Creator of the heavens and the earth, who hast entrusted to me the swift and solemn gift of life, be with me at this day's beginning. Thou art holy and wise and just and great, but Thou art also the loving Father of my spirit. Thou hast made me for a large purpose, so that I cannot crowd my life into a narrow space. Thou hast formed my heart to love Thee, my spirit to seek Thee, and my hands to serve Thee.

Forgive me that I have been unmindful of Thy presence— that when the freshness of the day has called to renewed dedication, I have risen and gone out to my work unheeding; that when the burning bush beside life's way has spoken of Thine unquenchable glory, I have not taken the shoes from off my feet. Forgive me my dullness, my selfishness, my fretful haste, my absorption with the lesser things and the temporary.

Open my eyes this day, that I may see Thee at every turn; quicken my ears that I may hear Thee speak; and stir my whole being with a glad response. *Amen.*

EVENING PRAYER

For the colours of the sky at the day's close I bless Thee; for the birds homing through the great spaces as the light dies away, and for the confidence of their strong wings I bless Thee. I bless Thee for every wild creature that seeks its rest and fulfilment as Thou hast appointed. I rejoice in the life and beauty of the world of Nature which Thou hast so wonderfully designed. But most of all, I rejoice in the limitless possibilities of the human spirit.

From olden times, men have turned aside at close of day, to seek Thy face; and my need of Thee today is the same. I need to turn my faltering steps to Thee—to lose my weakness in Thy mighty strength, to know Thy holy love without which I cannot live, and to feel Thy forgiveness. I need to hear again Thy gracious accents in the voice of Jesus, to see Thy redeeming purpose in His life. I need to know myself bound ever closer to others who also call Thee 'Father'.

Thou who didst raise Jesus Christ from the dead, and didst set Him at Thy right hand in glory everlasting, quicken within me the hope of immortality, that I may remember in whose likeness I am made, and in whose purpose I live and have my being. And to Thy name be the glory for ever, and ever.

Amen.

Praying Without Ceasing

READING: 1 Thessalonians 5^{17}

The farm was a happy place in which to grow up—with geese in the long grass, and great hams hanging in the back kitchen. Each Sunday night was an occasion. As children, we sprawled before the fire, and had stories, and coloured-in our texts. There was no church near.

One night stands out in memory. We had settled down to colour the Lord's Prayer—its letters outlined on an imitation canvas, that later it might be fit to hang upon the wall. For half an hour we were absorbed, heads bent and eyes busy. Then eyes were lifted. My work was greeted with admiration. I was the first to finish. And then, suddenly, my childish joy was shattered: 'Look!' someone cried. 'Look! She's missed out the full-stop!' And I had.

Never now can I forget that night. But with my adult years I have learned a new truth. To leave out the full-stop from that Prayer is no error; indeed, I must somehow contrive to leave it out—for that great Prayer was never meant to have a full-stop!

I might have learned the secret years earlier if I had known the old country parson Mrs Gaskell knew. At family prayers, night by night, he gathered around him his family and servants, and after he had faithfully fashioned petitions to embrace their needs, he remembered the cattle. One night he turned with concern to his serving-man kneeling at arm's length from him: 'John, didst see that Daisy had her warm mash tonight? For we must not forget the means, John. Two quarts of gruel, a spoonful of ginger—the poor beast needs it. . . . And here I am asking a blessing, and forgetting the means.'

In very truth, praying and serving are all of one piece. So the words of Scripture are plain to him who would see life whole: 'Pray without ceasing.' There is no place at the end of real prayer for a full-stop.

I see now that the most glorious judgement I can ever hope to hear on earth, or in heaven, is that which once troubled me: 'Look! She's missed out the full-stop!'

MORNING PRAYER

Gracious Father, let the words of my prayer and the service of my life be one this day.

Save me from cowardice that dare not face reality, from laziness that contents itself with half-truths, and from false piety that withdraws itself from men and things. Deliver me from all that is artificial, from all that is insincere, from all that is cloyed with pride. Keep my vision clear, my heart responsive, my will set on the highest. And, O Lord, teach me how to pray, that my prayer may serve Thy holy purpose in the world.

I commend to Thy Fatherly goodness all who have special need—those unable to set out upon this day's work with a glad heart and a light step; all those faced suddenly with some grave responsibility, with some unexpected change of plans, with some unguessed human weakness.

I commend to Thee all who enter on new work this day unsure of their capacities, uncertain about their reception, hesitant and fearful.

I commend to Thee all who in any way sow flowers in the place of weeds, and all teachers who quicken young minds with a love of things beautiful and strong and true.

For these, O Lord, hear my prayer, and let my cry come unto Thee. *Amen.*

EVENING PRAYER

Gracious Father, now when the day's work is at an end and the darkness draws about me, I would seek Thy face.

Like those who have sought thee, age after age, I live only by Thy grace. From Thee comes the very breath that I breathe, the power of my limbs, the sight of my eyes, the endless quest of my spirit. It is Thou who hast set me within the bounds of Time and Space, but the hurrying speed of life distracts me, till I almost forget that I am a child of Eternity. Forgive me that I have so often failed to find Thee in Thy gifts.

All the earth doth worship Thee, the Father everlasting. To Thee all angels cry aloud, the heavens and all the powers therein. To Thee cherubim and seraphim continually do cry:

Hymn. 22.

Prayer.

Hymn. 413.

Lesson. Mrs. Briggs

Solo ? Mrs Feggett

Promises. notices

Address, Mr Adair

Hymn 382.

Holy, holy, holy, Lord God of Sabaoth, heaven and earth are full of the majesty of Thy glory!

Let my praise, with that of all the redeemed, come unto Thee. Let my service be real, and unpretentious. Let my eyes be lighted with understanding, and my mouth be filled with kindness. Daily renew in me a sense of my Master's joy; for His name's sake. *Amen.*

As the Heart Aspires

READING: Isaiah 41⁶⁻⁷

It was pleasant in the warm sun. Forward and back Charlotte pushed the pram. The baby was asleep, but Charlotte was wider awake than usual. She held a book firmly in her hand.

Visitors sat in the park, and students from Harvard University near by walked through its peaceful ways. Nobody had ever taken much notice of Charlotte.

And then the unexpected happened. A smiling lady stepped toward her. 'Excuse me,' she said; 'you must not think me rude. But I could not help noticing your book. My name is Alice Freeman Palmer. I am President of Wellesley College. I have never before seen a girl try to learn Greek while she pushes a pram. I should be so interested to know why you do it.'

The face of the President of the famous college was so kind, and her speech so pleasant, that Charlotte found herself telling her dream. She had never told it to anyone before. And it seemed that her very voice took on a smile—a smile that seemed to show up the more because her face was black.

Charlotte wanted more than anything else in the world to be a teacher. It would not be easy. Her family was poor. But as she stood talking to the beloved President of Wellesley College it seemed that she could do anything.

When Charlotte was ready to go out into the world to teach, it was a little school among the poor down in Carolina that claimed her service. In those parts lived many Negro children who would always find it difficult to possess the treasure to be found in books. Any teacher who set out to teach them would have a battle to make the little school a success. But Charlotte was not afraid of a battle. And she did succeed.

True to her word that day in the park, Alice Freeman Palmer visited the tiny school and cheered its teacher. But even she could not know how gloriously the battle would be won. She could not know that there would come a day when the walls of the little school would be too small, when three hundred Negro children would come knocking.

So Charlotte Hawkins Brown, who had once tried to learn Greek, and the Alice Freeman Palmer Memorial Institute found an honoured place in the world. When asked how she had been able to do so much, and so well, Charlotte told of that far-away day in the park. Always her answer was the same: 'She loved me—she believed in me—I just had to succeed.'

MORNING PRAYER

Eternal Father, I thank Thee that Thou has not made us to walk a lonely way, but to know the encouragement and companionship of friends. I bless Thee for all that has been given to the world through friendship, for every high dream realized because another has shared it, for every wavering will made strong because a friend has stood by, for every difficulty met, and every joy doubled.

Teach me how to be a good friend. Give me warmth of heart and clarity of judgement; give me spontaneity and joy and dependability. Make me ready to bear the burdens of friendship—to share the difficult things and the disappointments, as well as the delights.

Bless all my friends—those near, and those whom I can see but seldom. Enrich us through the years, that we may have more to share with each other. Save us from looking inward upon ourselves; turn our eyes ever outward upon the world and the needs of others. Make our friendship fruitful in service.

May our friendship be more and more centred in Jesus, till His outreaching friendliness is ours. Give us His simplicity of heart, His honesty of mind, His greater eagerness to minister than to be ministered to, His serenity of spirit, and His unswerving devotion to Thy will; for His name's sake. *Amen.*

EVENING PRAYER

Holy, Holy, Holy, Lord God of Hosts,
Heaven and earth are full of Thy glory;
Glory be to Thee, O Lord most high!

I worship before Thy glory made manifest in Jesus Christ, I praise Thee for His humble village home and His kinship with working people; but above all for His Divine nature. His undying love.

I bless Thee for all who have striven to continue His service in lowly places. For the father and mother and poor mill home of David Livingstone, I bless Thee, and for his aspiring heart; for the early life and struggles of Mary Slessor, and for her undaunted courage; for Albert Schweitzer's simple home, and for his great gifts offered freely for Thy service.

Bless especially this night, I pray Thee, all men and women whose hearts are set on service, especially those who must overcome great obstacles. Sustain their courage, and bring others to their aid.

And by Thy mercy, enable us all, in the place where Thou hast set us, to present unto Thee our bodies and minds and spirits, a living sacrifice; for Jesu's sake. *Amen.*

He Loved Life

READING: 1 Corinthians 10$^{31-3}$

Young Alfred Sadd was an enthusiast. Perhaps it was partly that near his home at Wickham had once lived a minister with a curious name—Joseph Billio. Everything that that good man did, he did with such enthusiasm that he added a word to the language. Those who knew Alfred Sadd, had often to use that word—*he did everything like Billio*.

Early, Alfred fell in love with boats. The sailing barges which brought cargoes of timber to the Sadd yards were a constant reminder of the great outside world. All his heroes at school and Cheshunt College were men of boats—Chalmers, Tamate of the South Seas, John Williams. And when he offered for missionary work, it was to the South Seas that he went—to the Gilbert Islands, whose only link with the outside world was by boat.

Soon he was having all the adventures he wanted—blowing holes in a reef, building a house, sailing round the islands, translating Bible stories into the language of the people, fixing up a printing-press and a radio station, even performing a complex surgical operation. And he wrote home that he wouldn't be anywhere else for worlds!

Then came war. The Gilbert Islands were soon in the thick of it. Alfred was given the chance to leave, but he said: 'No! No! My duty is plainly here. I must stand by my people!'

What happened next is best told in the moving words of an old Gilbertese helper. 'All the people gathered on the west of the Church. . . . The Japs created fear. . . . Mr Sadd came hurrying along on his bicycle, and two soldiers went to meet him. They spread the Union Jack on the ground right in his path, but he did not tread on it. . . . He was taken to be tried. . . . The Union Jack was again spread out in his path so that he would tread on it, but Mr Sadd stooped down, took up the flag in his hands, gathered it and presented it to the officer. . . . The Japs marvelled at him.

'The decision was to go to Tarawa, and he was sent back to

get his clothes. . . . He saw me and said, '*Itaia Ti a leabo*' (Good-bye. We shall meet again).

'And next morning, a line was formed—Mr Sadd in the middle—and presently, Mr Sadd stood in front of them and spoke words of courage. And when he had finished, he went back and stood a little in front so that he would be the first to die. . . . And all the Europeans were happy and unafraid when they saw the courage of Mr Sadd.'

Today, on Tarawa, stands a tall simple cross, in memory of the man who did everything like Billio, and twenty-two others, British men who gave their lives. And that simple cross bears these everlasting words: 'Standing unarmed to their posts, they matched brutality with gallantry, and met death with fortitude.'

MORNING PRAYER

Eternal Father, I come before Thee at the beginning of this day, weak and mortal amidst the immensities of life. Show me what I am, and what I may become in Thy great purpose. Lift my eyes beyond the things of time and sense to issues which are eternal.

Forgive me if I have been half-hearted in Thy service. Forgive me if I have valued safety above the high, clear call.

> *God be in my head:*
> *And in my understanding;*
> *God be in mine eyes:*
> *And in my looking;*
> *God be in my mouth:*
> *And in my speaking;*
> *God be in my heart:*
> *And in my thinking;*
> *God be at mine end:*
> *And at my departing.*
> *Amen.*

EVENING PRAYER

O God of all brave men and women, I bless Thee this night for every splendid deed, for every high purpose made actual in shop and office and market-place, for the loving service of those at home, and for all who have shown courage this day. I bless Thee for every new thought, every new aspiration, every new task begun. Especially do I thank Thee for giving me the opportunity to share in this day's work.

As the night draws in, give me peace and rest.

Be with all who cannot sleep, and all who must work this night—nurses on duty and doctors, policemen, firemen, newspaper men, milkmen.

Bless all who must be far from home this night—the captains and crews of ships, engine-drivers and all who travel with them, men and women of the airways whose planes find their way through the night skies.

Bless those on duty in great factories, those who tend power-stations, prisoners and those who guard them within high walls.

For all who are lonely, I pray, and for all who are afraid. We are Thy children though frail and faltering and full of self. Forgive us, and grant us Thy peace. *Amen.*

Mind the Light

READING: Matthew 5^{14-16}

My journeying in America brought me nothing finer than the story of Kate Walker.

Mrs Walker, they said, never enjoyed talking about herself, she was shy. But after a time her story got out. 'I was living at Sandy Hook,' she said, 'when I met Jacob Walker. He kept the Sandy Hook Lighthouse. He took me there as his bride. Then we were transferred to Robin's Reef. It was a bleak place. At first I said: "I won't stay. The sight of water whichever way I look makes me lonesome." I refused to unpack my trunks and boxes. But as things were needed, they got unpacked.'

There was much to do in the lighthouse—brass to polish, lenses to clean, and lamps to trim. And when fog settled its clammy fingers around, there was a siren to sound or a bell to pound.

'By and by,' went on Kate Walker, 'my husband caught a heavy cold while tending the light. It turned to pneumonia, and he had to be taken to Smith Infirmary on Staten Island. That was two miles away.'

As she paused, it seemed that she could still see the little boat pitching and tossing that wild night at the foot of the ladder. 'I could not leave the light, of course,' she added. He understood. Then one night, whilst I sat tending the light, I saw a boat coming. Something told me the news it was bringing. Then the words came up to me through the darkness: "We are sorry, Mrs Walker, but your husband is worse."

' "He is dead," I said.

'We buried him in the little cemetery over on the hill. And every morning since, when the sun has come up, I have stood and looked in the direction of that grave. Sometimes there is snow over the hills and they are white. Sometimes they are green. But always I remember three words that I heard Jacob say more often than anything else in his life: "Mind the light!"'

Mrs Walker had grown white like those hills in winter, hearing those words. One and another had been appointed to help her, but no one ever stayed. 'Too lonely,' the first said. 'Too lonely.' And man after man echoed the words.

But Kate Walker heard other words echoing down the years, and she remained faithful—the only woman light-keeper—completely surrounded by treacherous seas.

MORNING PRAYER

O living Lord, I bless Thee that to ordinary men and women Thou didst entrust the light, saying: 'Let your light so shine before men that they may see your good works, and glorify your Father which is in heaven!'

> Direct, control, suggest, this day,
>   All I design, or do, or say,
> That all my powers, with all their might,
>   In Thy sole glory may unite.
>   Amen.

‍NG PRAYER

Thee, O God, for the night that comes quietly to
y eyes with sleep, and my limbs with rest. I thank
r the tasks of this day that is past.
d of many voices, who dost speak through the words
rophet, the poems of the psalmist, and the story of the
language is Thine, all music, all beautiful shapes and
and through them all Thou dost speak. Speak to me
ugh the silence of the night, and through adoration
ship.
for all who are lonely this night—for all lighthouse-
guarding the treacherous coast; for the aged whose
ers have gone on before; for those who are shy, slow
strangers and to make friends; for all who know the
s of responsibility. I pray for all doctors and nurses
onaries and evangelists who serve Thee far from their
e lands. I pray Thee for all whose work is difficult, or
s, or dull.
y friends wherever they are this night; guide them
the richest things of life. Bless those whose lot it is to

lead and guide the thought and life of others. Bless all teachers and leaders of boys and girls; all who serve unstintingly for the betterment of social conditions; all who, crippled or hindered through sickness, serve Thee through prayer and cheerful courage.

May Thy holy will be done, and Thy kingdom come in all our hearts. *Amen.*

His Word is Sure

READING: Matthew 25³⁴⁻⁴⁰

Each night the orphan boys in the home of good John Falk bowed their heads to say the simple grace that he had taught them: 'Lord Jesus, be our guest, and bless the food Thou hast provided.'

One night John Falk noticed that a little boy was looking mystified, and asked him why. 'Do tell me,' said the little boy, 'why He never comes. We ask every day, but He never comes.'

John Falk looked into the boy's eyes, and said very simply: 'Be sure of this. He does not despise our invitation.'

'Then,' said the little boy, 'I will set a place ready for Him,' and he ran to bring another stool to the table.

Even as he set the stool in place, there was a rap at the door. All the boys looked up, and then at each other, in surprise and expectancy.

John Falk himself rose and went to the door. There before him stood a broken soldier, weary and worn, finished with war, making his way home. He sought, he said, a night's lodging.

Without further words, he was brought in to join the simple meal. And he took, as seemed natural, the extra place at the table.

One boy offered his bread roll, another his mug of milk. Another begged him to have his bed for the night, and all the boys vied with one another in generous kindness to the stranger.

In the morning, as they gathered round at the rising of the sun to bid the soldier farewell, it seemed to them that they had never housed a stranger so happily. And only as good John Falk repeated to them some words of their Master did they so much as guess why: *'Inasmuch as ye have done it unto one of the least of these, ye have done it unto me.'*

MORNING PRAYER

Gracious Lord, I bless Thee for this new day, with its fresh opportunities for compassion.

For all who are homeless I pray, for all who this day must know peril, for all who must suffer pain. Surround all little children with Thy love, and give Thy wisdom and Thy patience to those who tend and teach them.

Bless all those who serve the common good—pastors, physicians, lawyers and merchants. And give Thy spirit to all in places of authority—social workers, and statesmen.

Deliver us this day from judging by material standards; let us not lose the eternal value of the individual in the crowd; let us take time to be kind, if need be at cost to ourselves; enable us to share gladly the good gifts of body, mind and estate with which Thou hast endowed us; and so this day make us show by our service the reality of our faith and love; for Jesu's sake. *Amen.*

EVENING PRAYER

Gracious Lord and Father, as the darkness closes in around me, my thoughts turn toward Thee.

I pray this night for all whose minds are darkened by distrust, by bitterness, by pride; for all who have been bruised by life, for all who find themselves bewildered. Be with all those who toss restless on their pillows, and with all who are in sorrow, and those who are distraught. Have mercy on Thy children and grant them Thy light, that they may find their way when life is darkened about them.

Let me have a care for those who are nobody's care—the orphans, the unloved, and the little ones robbed of the security of home by broken relationships. Let my love reach out to the aged, the dull, and the lonely. Give me the power to bring some added brightness into the lives of those with whom I live and work. Deliver me from dullness of conscience, from absorption in my own little affairs, from lack of imagination where others' interests are concerned. And deliver me from all self-consciousness, that my service may be done for the sake of my Lord and Master, and in His spirit. *Amen.*

esp. lonely. people walking alone on the streets. perhaps desperate. unable to unburden their hearts. Lord make thyself known to them. & help us to pray for them.

The Whole Earth Filled with His Glory

READING: Luke 9²⁸⁻³⁶

My conversion was an unforgettable experience—yet as difficult to catch in words as that experience on the mountain-side for Peter and James and John. They only knew they had been asleep, unseeing and unfeeling. And Jesus, the Son of God, had been at their side all the time. Then suddenly they were awake! '*And when they were awake, they saw His glory.*'

Masefield's Saul Kane, that one-time drunken prize-fighter, had a like experience. He, too, was unseeing, unfeeling—desperately unseeing, unfeeling—and then, unexpectedly and dramatically it happened at the word of a Quaker girl. And when he was awake he saw His glory. Though the words ran swiftly from his lips never could he tell the whole of it; he could only say:

> *The station brook to my new eyes*
> *Was bubbling out of paradise,*
> *The waters rushing from the rain*
> *Were singing 'Christ is risen again'.*
>
> *I thought all earthly creatures knelt*
> *From rapture of the joy I felt.*
> *The narrow station wall's brick ledge,*
> *The wild hop withering in the hedge,*
> *The lights in Huntsman's upper storey*
> *Were parts of an eternal glory.*

God pity the soul that has not such a moment. There is nothing to match it.

For me, at first, it might be His glory in Nature—His wild honeysuckle growing in the hedge. Had any honeysuckle smelled so sweet since the world began? Not for me. Had the sky ever been so blue, the clouds so light? Not for me. Everything was different. But supremely, I saw '*the glory of God* in the face of Jesus' (2 Corinthians 4⁶).

73

MORNING PRAYER

Eternal God, who art everywhere present, Thy purpose moving within the framework of this wondrous world and shining in our human spirits, I thank Thee that Thou dost never let us go and that in every age men and women have had dealings with Thee. Journeyings into far places have not taken them beyond Thy holy love, nor have the devious windings of their sinful hearts turned Thee aside from Thy purpose of redemption.

I bless Thee for Thy supreme revelation of Thyself in Jesus, for the experience of those who companied with Him in the days of His flesh, and for those loving hearts of each succeeding generation who have known him just as near.

Thou hast made us for full and glorious life. Stab my spirit broad awake this day, that I may see Thy glory and live. And quicken my sense of fellowship with all who share this great experience; for the sake of Jesus Christ, our Lord. *Amen.*

EVENING PRAYER

Eternal Father, in this quiet moment at the end of the busy day I, Thy child, rest in Thee.

Forgive me that I have allowed the clamour of the passing hour to invade the secret places of my spirit, that I have bartered quiet of mind for feverish haste and uncertainty, and have forgotten Thy glory revealed in the face of Jesus my Lord.

Restore to me the fresh wonder of my first wakening response to Thee, when the honeysuckle was sweeter, the sky bluer, and something of Thy divine purpose stood revealed in the face of every man and woman.

I bring to Thee my thanks for all physical joys; for the ecstasy of swift motion, for water, for hills and trees, for the good sound of rain on dry ground, for the stars set in the great spaces overhead, for music and song and every lovely thing.

Deliver me from all that would hinder me from sharing with others my living experience of Thee. *Amen.*

Whosoever Will Save His Life . . .

READING: Mark 8³⁵

There was no one quite like him—that gentle Indian in the saffron robe. Born into a rich and influential family, he grew up a member of a religious community, a Sikh of the Sikhs.

But now he wore his saffron robe as a sign of his new life. For his family had driven him forth, or more properly, his new faith had driven him forth on to the roads and the wild tracks. Men called him Sundar Singh. Some mistook him for the Christ when they heard that he had no place whereon to lay his head, and saw his quiet courage and gentleness and love.

Once, as he journeyed into Tibet, he had for company over the great mountain passes a Buddhist monk. The two had journeyed for hours in silence when they saw a storm approaching. They knew that if they could reach a certain monastery before dark all would be well; if not, they might die in the mountains. Together they hurried on, the icy wind seeming to search out the thin parts of their garments. Suddenly their eyes met questioningly. Was that a man groaning?

The two wayfarers moved to the edge of the roadway, and looked over. Their fears were confirmed. Far below lay a man, a poor broken thing. Night was fast coming on. Said the Buddhist: 'In my belief, this is Karma, the work of fate. This man's lot is to die here.'

'No,' said the Christian in the saffron robe; 'in my belief, this man is my brother, and he has need of me.'

So one man hurried on, holding his thin garment against the storm, and the other clambered down the hazardous slope. He reached the wretched man, and put him on his back. Then he struggled upwards on to the darkened road.

Under his burden, his thought all but numbed, he made his way to where the monastery lights shone through the storm. Then suddenly, when almost at his goal, his burden heavy upon him, he stumbled and fell. And next moment he knew the cause. In his way lay the huddled figure of the Buddhist frozen to death.

75

Weary and heated with his effort, he looked on in pity and wonder—and in that moment knew that he had escaped a like fate only because he had a brother in Christ.

MORNING PRAYER

Gracious Lord, I cannot tell what adventures will be mine this new day. I must meet with friends, work-fellows, and strangers. I cannot read the hidden secrets of their hearts, I cannot know all their need, I cannot alone meet the claims that at any moment they may lay upon me. But Thou art more than sufficient, and of Thy love and mercy there is no end.

Use me to minister to the needy, the distressed, and the discouraged this day. Use me to minister to the shy, the lonely and the distrustful. Use me, I pray Thee, to minister to the sick in body, the self-sufficient, and the proud.

Let the words of my Lord ring in my heart: 'Whosoever will save his life shall lose it: and whosoever will lose his life for My sake shall find it.'

Make me understanding toward people I don't like, and tolerant. Make me unself-conscious in my giving, that my right hand may not know what my left hand doeth. Moved by Love, true, strong and unflinching, let me serve only the Kingdom of my Lord—in His spirit, and for His sake. *Amen.*

EVENING PRAYER

Gracious Lord, though I speak with the tongues of men and of angels, and have not love, I am become as sounding brass, or a tinkling cymbal. And though I have the gift of prophecy, and understand all mysteries, and all knowledge; and though I have all faith, so that I could remove mountains, and have not love, I am nothing. And though I bestow all my goods to feed the poor, and though I give my body to be burned, and have not love, it profiteth me nothing.

Lord lead me into the way of this love, that reaching up to Thee, reaches out also to those who have need. Cleanse me of all self-seeking, smallness of vision, niggardliness of giving.

Turn my eyes outward from myself. Enable me to develop and consecrate what skills I have from Thee, that I may serve Thee better.

So make me an interpreter of Thy Divine Love that once walked this human way, ministering Thy mercy and Thy holiness; for His dear sake. *Amen.*

Each Heart hath Its Need

READING: Philippians 4¹⁹

The morning was fresh and bright, the sky blue, the bees busy in the clover. I pulled up at the little gate, and unlatched it. As I walked up the path I wondered what I should say to my friend—for she had gone blind. Blind! Never to see the face of a friend, never to feast the imagination on stately cloud-castles, never to see a daisy curtsy to a bee, or to watch the hay-stacks being piled up under the sun!

Usually we sat and talked of friends and of the things we had done, but this morning it was otherwise. Before we sat down, my old friend said: 'I have something to show you.' And she led the way through to her little kitchen. There on the only spare wall hung a fine copy of Holman Hunt's 'The Light of the World'.

'But why have you hung it in the kitchen?' I asked.

'Well, my dear,' she replied, 'this is where I feel the darkness most. I used to get such happiness out of my kitchen. I enjoyed the sun coming in each morning and the visit of the milkman, and I enjoyed my yellow crocks and the look of things tidy on the shelves. When the darkness came, this is where I needed courage most.'

In that moment it seemed there was light in that little kitchen. My eyes lingered on that Figure of 'The Light of the World' standing with kingly mien, knocking.

'You like this of Him?' she asked. 'It's lovely, isn't it?'

'Yes,' I replied, 'it is very lovely indeed'—adding, under my breath—'and to one in the darkness, loveliest of all!'

MORNING PRAYER

Eternal Christ, Thou art the Light of the world, and in Thy presence is no darkness.

Thou knowest the need of my heart better than I know it myself, and Thou art able to meet that need today.

But I have need of which I do not know. Come near, and touch my life into new beauty and joy. Banish the darkness of self-sufficiency. Shine into my inmost being with Thy light of love and faith and hope.

> *Dear Master, in whose life I see*
> *All that I would, fail to be,*
> *Let Thy clear light for ever shine,*
> *To shame and guide this life of mine.*
>
> *Though what I dream and what I do*
> *In my weak days are always two,*
> *Help me, oppressed by things undone,*
> *O Thou, whose deeds and dreams were one!*
> *Amen.*

EVENING PRAYER

O God, my Father, I rejoice that in the beginning Thy word was 'Let there be light!'—that Thou hast never ceased to say to the minds and hearts of men and women.

I bless Thee for Jesus, the Light of the world—for His humanity and His holy love. I bless Thee for His divine patience, that He stands knocking. So easily He might have overwhelmed my poor powers, and gained entrance by force. So easily He might have disregarded my gift of choice, and compelled me to receive Him. But He has chosen to stand and knock. Such humility, such love are beyond all human understanding.

Let every part of this day's labour and leisure that will not bear His light be cast away. Forgive me for any lowered ideals, any envious thoughts, any hasty words. Forgive me if I have allowed pride to rule my actions, or intolerance my judgements. Forgive me if I have wasted the precious hours of the day. Teach me to live every hour as in Thy presence, that both my work and my leisure, justly joined, may be to Thine honour and glory.

Let the healing and forgiving Jesus banish all that would take peace from my mind as I come to rest. I have no light of my own to lighten my way, or to direct my will, but by Thy mercy, I have no need to walk in darkness. *Amen.*

Sorrow Transformed

READING: Psalm 40[3]

Beside the grand piano she stood, tall and gracious, her eyes closed. And her voice reached every heart. She was singing one of her favourite spirituals:

> Go tell it on the mountain,
> Over the hills and everywheah;
> That Jesus Christ is aborn.

But for that shining reality, life for Marian Anderson—as for her people up through the long years—must have been very different. Through the helpful influence of her father and mother she came to that faith early. At thirteen she was singing in the choir; at fifteen her formal training began; at sixteen she gave her first important concert; and always her life was merged with that of her people, so that she sang their songs fashioned out of life.

In 1924, Marian Anderson won the right to appear with the New York Orchestra—an honour richly prized. Six years later she studied in Germany. Applause greeted her all the way. As she sang through Norway and Finland, Sibelius paid her the highest compliments. Toscanini, at the Austrian Musical Festival, said to her: 'Yours is a voice such as one hears once in a hundred years.' Her fame seemed assured; many a young singer might have lost her head—but not Marian Anderson. She recognized her deep allegiance to God and to her people. Her chosen songs were the spirituals, and her favourite among them was the 'Crucifixion'.

At her concerts on the Continent many who sought to hear her in crowded halls had to be turned away, and a like experience was hers in South America. Only when she returned to her own country did an ugly incident mar her glorious service. In Washington she was to sing in the Constitution Hall—owned and controlled by the Daughters of the American Revolution. Despite the admirable efforts of several groups, the use of the Hall was refused.

But the slight to the coloured singer and her people had a number of surprising results. At once Eleanor Roosevelt, first lady in the land, resigned her membership of the organization, and the night planned for the concert, Marian Anderson sang in the open air, in front of Lincoln's Memorial, to a vast concourse of people who could never have got into the Hall.

The distinguished singer herself had no comment to make— but she suffered. There was no doubt about that. Only later did she add very calmly: 'Religion helps one to face the difficulties one sometimes meets.'

MORNING PRAYER

O Thou who hast parted the daylight from the dark, and caused the sun to shine and the rain to fall upon the just and the unjust, I rejoice in this new day. Let me enter into it as into a gift from Thee.

I bless Thee for the world family of which I am a part— so rich and so diverse. I bless Thee for Him, in whose kingdom there is neither Greek nor Jew, barbarian nor Scythian, bond nor free, male nor female, and I give Thee thanks that all may own Him Saviour and Lord, and all may bring to Him loving service.

Never let me forget that He was born of a simple Hebrew mother; that He ministered first, in Thy good purpose, to the house of Israel; that He was quick to rejoice in the faith of a Syrophœnician woman and a Roman centurion; that as He trod the sorrowful way His cross was carried by a man with a black skin.

Quicken my memory of these things—and forgive my racial prejudices. Forbid that I should despise any for whom Christ died, or that by word, or action, I should injure any in whom His Spirit lives. *Amen.*

EVENING PRAYER

Most merciful, Father, who hast called us to seek Thy face and to walk Thy way together, grant us Thy forgiveness that we are so slow to respond, and that we misuse Thy gifts, mar Thy work, and put stumbling-blocks in each other's way.

Grant us a vision of our land free of bitterness, a land of brotherhood where vice and poverty cease to fester, and where men and women rejoice equally in the light of the sun.

Help us to translate our love for the world family into the language of daily life, through our conversations and casual contacts, as well as in the deep places of thought and judgement.

O God, if we have prayed the prayer that our Lord taught us so easily and so often that its words have lost their challenge for us, teach us how to pray it not only with our lips, but with our lives, for His sake:

Our Father, which art in heaven . . . *Amen.*

The God of Common Things

READING: Psalm 8¹

Seemingly, people did not spend money for a picture of peasants whom they could see any day in the fields, and the peasant artist could not know that one day his picture would draw people from the ends of the earth. It was such a simple thing.

From early dawn the peasant folk laboured without pause till the calling of the Angelus bell. Jean François Millet knew the heart of the men and women he had put on to his canvas— he knew their slow speech and long endurance. They wore simple clothes, and moved as if clodded to the earth. But they were more than peasants of the Normandy fields; they were God's men and women.

Yet nobody wanted to buy his picture. And he would be almost sixty before someone came by with a thousand francs. Only after his life had ended would men and women waken to the inward significance of his figures. Then fame would come. But perhaps the artist did not need fame.

In time, the little picture of the Angelus would find its way out into the world. Long after the Belgian had stopped to exchange his francs for it, someone would covet it for 38,000 francs. Later still, it would cross the Atlantic for 553,000 francs. And only when a Frenchman, fulfilling a dream, could find 800,000 francs, would it come back to the country that gave birth to its artist, and to its peasant man and woman.

It was a small picture; some found fault with it for that. But size had never mattered to the artist.

From earliest childhood his mother had influenced his spirit. Morning after morning she had stood at her little boy's bedside, to say gently, 'Wake up, little François; the birds have been singing the glory of God for a long time!' In the evenings he had usually gone into the fields with his father. There he had learned to know himself rich in the things that money could never buy nor poverty take away. Never would he forget one evening, when, seated together, he and his father watched the sunset and the birds flying homeward. The sun set that night with a special glory. And all at once, Pére Millet rose and, baring his head, said: '*My son, it is God!*'

Jean François Millet was denied wealth; but he was not poor. No man can be poor who loves God and sees Him in life's common things!

MORNING PRAYER

O God, I bless Thee for this wondrous world—for the freshness of the morning, calling to new ventures; for the challenge of the midday with its burdens; for the sweet calm of the evening hour; and for the rest of night.

I bless Thee for every living thing that reveals Thy creative plan, for the might of the sun and stars and the majesty of the mountains. I bless Thee for the breaking bud and the bird on topmost bough. I bless Thee for the dumb creatures of the fields, and for their service to life.

I bless Thee for little children, and their dependence. I bless Thee for men and women of humble heart, whether they toil in lowly ways or in great places of responsibility. I bless Thee for all painters and poets and craftsmen, who bring to the common material things of earth a hint of Thy lasting beauty and truth.

For the gift of wonder and the joy of discovery I give Thee thanks, and for every fresh experience of Thy presence. The world in which Thou hast set me is for ever speaking; make me ready to harken for Thy voice in it all.

> *Lord of all being, throned afar,*
> *Thy glory flames from sun and star;*
> *Centre and soul of every sphere,*
> *Yet to each loving heart how near.*
> > *Amen.*

EVENING PRAYER

I will sing unto Thee, O Lord, a new song. I will bless Thy name, and show forth Thy salvation from day to day.

I will declare Thy glory among the heathen and Thy wonders among all people.

84

For Thou art great, and greatly to be praised; Thou art to be feared above all gods.

Honour and majesty are before Thee; strength and beauty are in Thy sanctuary.

I will give unto Thee glory and strength. I will bring my offering and come into Thy courts. I will worship Thee in the beauty of holiness.

O gracious Lord, hear my prayer. Grant me Thy rich blessing, and with the night, quiet rest; for Jesu's sake.

Amen.

Scholar into Friend

READING: John 15¹⁴

Tilak's mother was always at hand to encourage him in his boyhood's school, to share her deeply religious nature and her poetic gifts.

And then a day came when a doubt took root in his young heart. He had been sent to carry the offering to the family shrine. On the way, boylike, he had begun to nibble it. It proved tasty. So he broke off another portion and another until, too late, afraid at his daring, he had arrived at the shrine with an empty platter. What would the gods do? Perhaps they would strike him dead. And all that day he waited—and the next—but there was no response. And the small doubt that had taken root grew into a great doubt.

As time passed, Tilak saw about him the high-born and the miserable untouchables. And he knew that his country could never be great with that cruel contrast. Then, pondering deeply, he met a Christian missionary. They travelled together in a train. Before they took leave of each other, Tilak accepted the gift of a Book.

It was the turning-place for Tilak. 'In those chapters,' said he, with a new light in his dark brown eyes, 'I found an answer to the most abstruse problems of Hindu philosophy. And I found my heart's new Master.'

Persecution followed. But did persecution matter? His work was taken away. But did the loss of work matter? Tilak had found a new work—a new wonder, and a new song. 'Christ's scholar' had put himself to school once more. Though his wife and family at first looked on him with shame, the day would surely come, he believed, when they would join in service of the great Master. And his faith was no empty thing.

Through the Marathi Mission, all up and down the land, in the crowded places he served until, in 1919, he fell upon sleep.

Now his new song has found an echo in many a heart:

> One who is all unfit to count
>   As scholar in Thy school,
> Thou of Thy love hast named a friend—
>   O kindness wonderful!

MORNING PRAYER

O Lord, I bless Thee for the call of Christ that sounds in every age. I bless Thee that in my day that call is not one whit less insistent and challenging. Let me hear it again this morning, in the quietness of my heart.

What is unresponsive in me, do Thou kindle; what is stupid in me do Thou make wise; for His sake. *Amen.*

EVENING PRAYER

O Lord of Truth, before whom all that is hollow and unreal is done away, let the words of my lips, and the love of my heart be acceptable in Thy sight. This night I rejoice in Thy power, and rest in Thy mercy.

The voice of the seasons and the common things of every day speak of Thy faithfulness. The history of the past and the history that is being made today speaks of Thy righteousness. But above all is Thy holy love, seen most clearly in the face of Jesus.

His life gives meaning to all my comings and goings; His truth shines like a clear steady light; His presence transforms the lowliest task and the loneliest hour.

In this quietness, made solemn by remembrance of His cross, I dedicate myself anew. *Amen.*

Eyes of the Heart

READING: 1 Timothy 1⁵

I knew Kay well; we were fellow-students, and she was the favourite of us all. It wasn't that she had a better start or came from a better home. She didn't. Her parents were plain country-folk wresting a living from a poor farm. It wasn't as if Kay had more brains. She hadn't. It was just that she had something that we couldn't give a name to. It wasn't just the common power that makes a country girl into a princess—not that at all. It was something like imagination, but not the ordinary kind—it was the power to see and know how things would look and sound to other people. Kay had the happy faculty of looking at life from the inside.

If Kay set a tray for someone coming from a late lecture, it was unlike anyone else's tray—there was the same fresh cloth and cup-and-saucer—but the result was always quite different, quite personal. If Kay took a message over the 'phone, it never seemed a loss to receive it second-hand—for Kay had the happiest way with words, as with everything.

I didn't see her much after our college days—we moved to different parts of the country. But ten years later I was guest at Kay's wedding.

Kay and Alec have a family about them now. I met Alec by chance in town lately; we talked, and of course our talk was of Kay. Though I never see her now, I like to think of her in the midst of her home and family. She ought to be surrounded by young folk, with that secret of hers—the world needs nothing so much. There are so many crude, blunt powers in life today, that we need the ministry that a Christian imagination makes possible—the gift of saying and doing beautiful things beautifully. Kay still retains that secret. I know, for Alec had a brown-paper parcel under his arm. 'Just the usual little present,' said he smiling, when I drew his attention to it. 'But I couldn't run any risk. I might not be up in town again before January 2nd.' Then, after a pause, he added, 'I always remember the date because it's the day *after* New Year's

88

Day, but Kay never puts it like that—she says, "I remember New Year's Day only because it's the day before our wedding day." '

MORNING PRAYER

O Loving Father, who didst give to Jesus the power to open the eyes of the unseeing, open my eyes. Give me to see the beauty of the earth about me and the beauty of others' lives. Quicken my imagination that I may see with the eyes of my heart. Give me strength to help, gentleness, and understanding, as I go on my way.

I bless Thee for those whose lives touch mine. I bless Thee for those who have been at pains to see life from my point of view, for those who have rejoiced to give me pleasure, for those who have strengthened my belief in my own capacities.

I bless Thee for those who have written the books I love, and for those who have painted the pictures that bring beauty to my days. I bless Thee for those who have held out hands of compassion; for ministers, teachers, and dreamers.

I bless Thee for my home—for all who serve me there, and all who have claims upon me.

Help me to work as hard and play as fair in Thy sight alone, as if all the world saw. When I must do some tedious or unpleasant task, give me the grace of cheerfulness. Save me from walking rough-shod over the rights of others. Let no one with whom I have to do, nor any surprise, nor any accident, move me to anger. Show in my life, as in the Gospel story, the secret of my Master's courtesy. Make me ready to help others at cost to myself; and to Thy Name be all the glory, for ever and ever. *Amen.*

EVENING PRAYER

Most merciful Lord, Thou hast loved me with an everlasting love; Thou hast forgiven me, led me, disciplined me; Thou hast never despaired of me, even when I have despaired of myself. Always I have heard Thy voice leading me on, and leaning upon Thy strength, I have found it more than sufficient.

Forgive me that ever the song has died out of my days; forgive me that ever my mind has lost its daring, or my heart its courage.

I lay before Thee all that is precious to me—all that I have, all that I am, or can ever hope to be. I lay before Thee all my secret thoughts and my dearest wishes. Quicken me in Thy loving service.

In trust this night, as the darkness draws around me, I take my rest. As the stars come out in the quiet sky, and the night winds cool the heated and weary earth, so do Thou bless me with Thy gift of peace and renewal. *Amen.*

Servant of the Centuries

READING: John 5³⁹

It all went back to old Leipzig, and to the moment when a young student set out to be a New Testament scholar. At thirty, the university accepted his services as a professor, and the great world was before him. From city to city he journeyed, searching for ancient manuscripts.

Then came the memorable visit to St Catherine's Monastery, Mount Sinai. There, in one of the dusty depositories, lay a basket of parchments. What did the monks intend to do with them? No one had asked that question before. The eyes of the young scholar lightened with a new fascination as he turned them over, and when he went away he carried with him forty of those old parchment leaves. Soon the world of scholarship was agog with the wonder of Tischendorf's discovery.

But fifteen long years were to pass before he set foot in the Monastery again. On his second visit he carried a commission for search from the Emperor of Russia; but careful search yielded nothing of significance. Only on the last night, as Tischendorf shared a simple meal with the kindly old steward, did there come light into his eyes. Casually, as the two men sat at table, the old steward lifted from a cupboard a bundle of ancient manuscripts wrapped in red cloth. Tischendorf watched with curious interest as the steward undid the wrappings. Late that night his host allowed him to take the manuscripts away to his sleeping-place to turn over at will. Those 390 leaves of ancient vellum proved to be a priceless find—a *Fourth-Century manuscript* of the whole of the New Testament, and part of the Old.

Soon, lovers of the Scriptures all over the world heard the news. It meant that new light, through scholarship, was thrown upon the glorious business of living. Today, the greater part of Tischendorf's discovery—the *Codex Sinaiticus* —is treasured in the British Museum for the service it can render. So, in the kindly light of Eternal Purpose, the young student from Leipzig was allowed to be a servant of the centuries!

MORNING PRAYER

O Lord, I bless Thee for good men inspired by Thy Spirit, for scholars and martyrs and translators who have made it possible for me to read the Bible. I bless Thee for all who have served Thee with patience to make clear its meaning, and for all Christian men and women in high and in low places who have lived by its shining truth.

I pray for the great Societies that publish and circulate this Book today, so that the least of us may know it, and the poorest possess it.

I pray for all who collect money for its publication, and all who give time and strength.

> *O Word of God incarnate,*
> *O Wisdom from on high,*
> *O Truth unchanged, unchanging,*
> *O Light of our dark sky,*
> *We praise Thee for the radiance*
> *That from the hallowed page,*
> *A lantern to our footsteps,*
> *Shines on from age to age.*
> *Amen.*

EVENING PRAYER

O Lord, the day is done, but with Thee there is no darkness. Thou art the Eternal Light.

I bless Thee for Thy sustaining love this day and for the many ways in which Thou hast made it known to me: in the handclasp of a friend, the trust of little children, the loveliness of flowers and trees, and the shining truth of Thy written Word.

I bless Thee for the courage of ordinary people, for the skill of craftsmen, and the consecrated minds of scholars. I bless Thee for those who make the music of our world and those who teach us the value of silence. I bless Thee for the experience of age and for the eagerness of youth. I bless Thee for all who serve our lives in simple ways.

I bless Thee still more for the world within—higher and deeper than yet I know, and more wonderful—the kingdom of the mind and spirit. I stand awed in Thy presence. I marvel that Thou hast made me.

Teach me how to live; save me from a daily servitude to things; deliver me from the narrow prison of pride; let me remember constantly the claims of others; and keep the edges of my mind clean.

Whether I wake or sleep, in Thee alone do I live and move and have my being. *Amen.*

Across the Valley

READING: John 8¹²

A measure of satisfaction for some was in the great city, but
the story-teller soon wearied and sought out for himself a little
house on the side of a valley.

One day, after he had been there for some time, he went a
walk to the other side. At a lonely farmhouse he came upon a
woman. She was shy—few strangers came that way. But
presently, she said a memorable thing, and Kipling the story-
teller never forgot it: 'Be you the new light 'crost the valley
yonder? You don't know what a comfort you've been to me
this winter. You aren't ever goin' to shroud 'em up—or
be ye?'

Most of us learned early the twenty-third Psalm—about 'the
Valley of the Shadow'. There might be some who would
question what the words meant to the Psalmist: but we know
what they mean to us. Since the Psalmist's day, *a New Light
has been set across the Valley!*

That is the glory of our faith. Our attitude to Death is
transformed by the knowledge that there is One on the Other
Side. That does not answer all our questions, but it does give
us the satisfaction known to the old saint who confessed:

> *My knowledge of that life is small,*
> *The eye of faith is dim;*
> *But 'tis enough that Christ knows all,*
> *And I shall be with Him.*

Once—locating God in Time—a Cross was raised up, and
a garden tomb sealed. But in that garden on the third day, He
rose again. That fact changed the cowardice of a little handful
of disciples into glorious courage—and makes all the difference
today. So we teach it to our children, and we whisper it to
those who come to the end of the way:

'Don't be afraid,' we say. 'The Valley may appear dark—
but He has crossed it. He is the New Light across the Valley.
Never fear.'

MORNING PRAYER

O Lord of Life, I bless Thee for the world's first Easter morning. I remember those who were last at the Cross and earliest at the Tomb. I rejoice in the discovery of those who sped first to tell the Resurrection story to the world.

I marvel at Thy love that will never let me go. Dispel the darkness of my sin, that when I come to the last valley, it may be with courage and a quiet mind.

I praise Thee that across the Valley there is a New Light, even Jesus Christ, my Lord; that Death leads but to Life; that weeping may endure for a night, but joy cometh in the morning.

I pray for all who share this glorious faith, and for all who for want of it walk in darkness; for all who are sick, and lonely, and afraid; for all who have grown cynical and have lost their way; and especially for all who must meet Death this day—in their own experience, or in the passing of their dear ones.

Be close to me when I come to the parting of the ways. Strengthen my faith in the Life everlasting, and my love for the Lord of Life, triumphant for evermore. *Amen.*

EVENING PRAYER

Gracious Father, grant me Thy blessing at the day's close. I have been busy with my own small concerns, and have spared too little thought for the things which are eternal. Forgive me.

I have seen Thy glory in the morning sun and the arching skies; I have marked Thy majesty in the mountains and in the mind of man; I have beheld Thy tenderness in little children and in the wild flowers beside the way. The birds have shown me Thy joy and the streams Thy generosity. And still I have been slow to worship Thee. Forgive me.

I have been free to read the Scriptures, and to see there the love and strength and grace of Jesus. I have talked with men and women, and seen in their lives Thine eternal goodness. And still I have been slow to speak Thy name and to do Thy service. Forgive me.

Deliver me from self-importance and self-absorption. Lead me out of my littleness into Thy great and holy purpose

where is perfect freedom. Let me delight to do Thy will.
Give me a humble spirit. And lead me into Life Everlasting
for Jesu's sake, who lives and reigns for evermore. *Amen.*

So shall I know more fully Him whom I love and serve.
So shall I become here and now His interpreter.